Acclaim for
THE ONE WORLD SCHOOLHOUSE

"I discovered Sal Khan and Khan Academy like most other people—by using these incredible tools with my own kids. Sal Khan's vision and energy for how technology could fundamentally transform education is contagious. He's a true pioneer in integrating technology and learning. I'm happy that, through this book, even more people will be introduced to this groundbreaking innovator."

—Bill Gates, cofounder and chairman, Microsoft Corp

"[A] must-read for all who are committed to improving education so students everywhere can gain the skills and knowledge to be successful in school, careers, and life."

—George Lucas, filmmaker and founder, George
Lucas Educational Foundation, publisher of *Edutopia*

"The world dreams of education reform, and Sal Khan is delivering."

—Chris Anderson, TED (Technology,
Entertainment, Design) curator

"Sal Khan is changing what we believe is possible in education. You'll adore this book because it's just like his lessons—approachable, good-hearted, smart, and ultimately profound.

—Ted Mitchell, president and CEO,
NewSchools Venture Fund

"When you read this book, you will understand how the dignity of each student is addressed by education's visionary, Sal Khan."   —Ann Doerr, philanthropist

"Sal Khan has developed the best and most cost-efficient way to use technology to bring universal high-quality education, creativity, and innovation to *all*." —Carlos Slim Helú

Acclaim from KHAN ACADEMY USERS

"The power of what Sal Khan created cannot be overstated."
—Daniel Stern, co-founder of UConnect.org

"The most powerful and accessible learning model in the world."
—Jerry Hennessy, co-founder of BJ's restaurants

"Sal Khan has literally changed my life and the outcome of my grades." —Taylor

"I never would have even known that I love math and that I'm very good at it!" —Jordan

"You and your team are revolutionizing the way a top-level education can be provided." —Timothy

"If I keep up at this pace, I'll be at calculus in a little less than a year! Thank you, Angels of Math!" —Anonymous

"Maybe I could have done it without Khan, but this is the ace up my sleeve. Here's to free, accessible knowledge!" —Scot

"You've opened doors for us that we would have never been able to unlock alone." —Paesan

"Revolutionary. I really think it's going to be one of the most important contributions of my generation." —Denise

THE ONE WORLD SCHOOLHOUSE

EDUCATION REIMAGINED

SALMAN KHAN

TWELVE

NEW YORK   BOSTON

Twelve
Hachette Book Group
237 Park Avenue
New York, NY 10017

www.HachetteBookGroup.com

Printed in the United States of America

RRD-C

First trade edition: September 2013
10 9 8 7 6 5 4 3 2 1

Twelve is an imprint of Grand Central Publishing.
The Twelve name and logo are trademarks of Hachette Book Group, Inc.

The Hachette Speakers Bureau provides a wide range of authors for speaking events. To find out more, go to www.hachettespeakersbureau.com or call (866) 376-6591.

The publisher is not responsible for websites (or their content) that are not owned by the publisher.

The Library of Congress has cataloged the hardcover edition as follows:

Khan, Salman, 1976-
    The one world schoolhouse : education reimagined / Salman Khan.
        p. cm.
    Summary: "The founder of the Khan Academy—the world's most popular free online learning site—tells the story of his school's astonishing success, and shares his revolutionary vision for the future of education."—Provided by the publisher
    Includes bibliographical references and index.
    ISBN 978-1-4555-0838-9 (hardback)—ISBN 978-1-4555-0839-6 (ebook)
    1. Internet in education. 2. Education and globalization. 3. Self-culture. I. Title.
    LB1044.87.K485 2012
    371.33'44678
                                2012025840

ISBN 978-1-4555-0837-2 (pbk.)

CONTENTS

PART 3: INTO THE REAL WORLD

PART 4: THE ONE WORLD SCHOOLHOUSE

Don't limit a child to your own learning, for he was born in another time.

—RABINDRANATH TAGORE

The elements of instruction . . . should be presented to the mind in childhood, but not with any compulsion. Knowledge which is acquired under compulsion has no hold on the mind. Therefore do not use compulsion, but let early education be rather a sort of amusement; this will better enable you to find out the natural bent of the child.

—PLATO, THE REPUBLIC

THE ONE WORLD
SCHOOLHOUSE

Introduction

A Free, World-Class Education for Anyone, Anywhere

My name is Sal Khan. I'm the founder and original faculty of the Khan Academy, an institution serious about delivering a free education to anyone, anywhere, and I'm writing this book because I believe that the way we teach and learn is at a once-a-millennium turning point.

The old classroom model simply doesn't fit our changing needs. It's a fundamentally passive way of learning, while the world requires more and more *active* processing of information. The old model is based on pushing students together in age-group batches with one-pace-fits-all curricula and hoping they pick up something along the way. It isn't clear that this was the best model one hundred years ago; it certainly isn't anymore. Meanwhile, new technologies offer hope for more effective ways of teaching and learning, but also engender confusion and even fear; too often the shiny new technology is used as little more than window dressing.

Between the old way of teaching and the new, there's a crack in the system, and kids around the globe are falling through it every day. The world is changing at an ever faster rate, yet systemic change, when it happens at all, moves glacially and often in the wrong direction; every day—every class period—the gap grows wider between the way kids are being taught and what they actually need to learn.

All of this is easily said, of course. For better and worse, everyone is talking about education these days. Politicians bring it up in every speech. Parents worry aloud that their children are falling behind relative to some vague, mysterious, yet powerful set of standards, or being shown up by a competitor two rows over or halfway around the world. As in arguments about religion, there are fiercely held opinions, often in the absence of verifiable proof. Should kids have more structure or less? Are we testing too little or too much? And speaking of tests, do the standardized exams measure durable learning or just a knack for taking standardized exams? Are we promoting initiative and comprehension and original thinking, or just perpetuating an empty game?

Adults worry on their own behalf as well. What happens to our capacity to learn once our formal education is finished? How can we train our minds so they don't become lazy and brittle? Can we still learn new things? Where and how?

All this talk about education is healthy in that it affirms the absolutely central importance of learning in our competitive and connected world. The problem is that it has not translated into improvement. Where there is action, it often is top-down government policies that are as likely to hurt as help. There are amazing teachers and schools who have shown that excellence is possible, but their success has proven hard to replicate and scale. Despite all the energy and money spent on the problem, the progress dial has barely budged. This has led to a deep cynicism about whether education can be systemically improved at all.

Even more troubling, many people seem somehow to overlook the basic fact of what the crisis is about. It's not about graduation rates and test scores. It's about what those things mean to the outcome of human lives. It's about potential realized or squandered, dignity enhanced or denied.

It is often cited that American high school students now rank twenty-third in the world in science and math proficiency. From a U.S.-centric perspective, that's distressing; but these tests are a very narrow measure of what is happening in a country. I believe that, for the near future at least, the United States will maintain its leadership position in science and technology *despite* any potential failings in our school system. Alarmist rhetoric aside, the United States is not about to lose its primacy because students in Estonia are better at factoring polynomials. Other aspects of U.S. culture—a unique combination of creativity, entrepreneurship, optimism, and capital—have made it the most fertile ground in the world for innovation. That's why bright kids from all around the globe dream of getting their green cards to work here. From a global, forward-looking perspective, the national rankings are also somewhat beside the point.

But if alarmism is uncalled for, complacency would be downright disastrous. There's nothing in American DNA that gives us a lock on entrepreneurship and invention, and our leadership position can only erode if we fail to keep it propped up with fresh and well-schooled minds.

Even while America remains a powerhouse of innovation, who will benefit from it? Will only a small fraction of American students have the education they need in order to participate, forcing U.S. companies to import the balance of talent? Will a large and growing percentage of America's own young people remain un- or underemployed because they lack the necessary skills?

The same questions need to be asked on behalf of youth all around the world. Will their potential be squandered or channeled in dangerous directions because they weren't given the tools or the opportunity to grow the economic pie? Will real democracy in the developing world fail to gain a foothold because of bad schools and a corrupt or broken system?

These questions have both practical and moral dimensions. It's my belief that each of us has a stake in the education of *all* of us. Who knows where genius will crop up? There may be a young girl in an African village with the potential to find a cancer cure. A fisherman's son in New Guinea might have incredible insight into the health of the oceans. Why would we allow their talents to be wasted? How can we justify *not* offering those children a world-class education, given that the technology and resources to do so are available—if only we can muster the vision and the boldness to make it happen?

But instead of acting, people just keep talking about incremental changes. Either for lack of imagination or fear of rocking the boat, the conversation generally stops well short of the kind of fundamental questioning that our educational malaise demands, focusing instead on a handful of familiar but misplaced obsessions like test scores and graduation rates. Those are by no means trivial concerns. Still, what really matters is whether the world will have an empowered, productive, fulfilled population in the generations to come, one that fully taps into its potential and can meaningfully uphold the responsibilities of real democracy.

As we address this, we will revisit fundamental assumptions. How do people actually learn? Does the standard classroom model—broadcast lectures in school, solitary homework in the evening—still make sense in a digital age? Why do students forget so much of what they have supposedly "learned" as soon as an exam has been taken? Why do grown-ups sense such a disconnect between what they studied in school and what they do in the real world? These are the sorts of basic questions we should be asking. But even then, there is an enormous difference between bemoaning the state of education and actually doing something about it.

In 2004—somewhat by accident, as I'll explain—I started experimenting with some ideas that seemed to be working. To a large degree, they were new incarnations of well-proven principles. On the other hand, coupled with the scalability and accessibility of new technologies, they pointed to the possibility of rethinking education as we know it.

Of the various experiments, the one that took on a life of its own was my posting of math lessons on YouTube. I didn't know how best to do this, or if it would work at all, or if anyone would watch what I posted. I proceeded by trial and error (yes, errors are allowed) and within the time constraints imposed by a rather demanding day job as a hedge fund analyst. But within a few short years it had become clear to me that my passion and my calling were in virtual teaching; in 2009, I quit my job to devote myself full-time to what had by then morphed into the Khan Academy.

If the name was rather grand, the resources available to this new entity were almost comically meager. The Academy owned a PC, $20 worth of screen capture software, and an $80 pen tablet; graphs and equations were drawn—often shakily—with the help of a free program called Microsoft Paint. Beyond the videos, I had hacked together some quizzing software running on my $50-per-month web host. The faculty, engineering team, support staff, and administration consisted of exactly one person: me. The budget consisted of my savings. I spent most of my days in a $6 T-shirt and sweatpants, talking to a computer monitor and daring to dream big.

I didn't dream of creating a popular website or of being a flash-in-the-pan entry in the education debate. Maybe I was delusional, but I dreamed of creating something enduring and transformative, an institution for the world that could last hundreds of years and help us fundamentally rethink how schooling might be done.

The time was right, I thought, for such a fundamental reexamination. New educational institutions and models emerge at inflection points in history. Harvard and Yale were founded shortly after the colonization of North America. MIT, Stanford, and the state university systems were products of the Industrial Revolution and American territorial expansion. We are now still in the early stage of an inflection point that

I believe is the most consequential in history: the Information Revolution. And in this revolution, the pace of change is so swift that deep creativity and analytical thinking are no longer optional; they are not luxuries but survival skills. We can no longer afford for only some part of the world's population to be deeply educated. With those things in mind, I composed a mission statement that was both wildly ambitious and—with the help of readily available but absurdly underutilized technology—completely attainable: Provide a free, world-class education for anyone, anywhere.

My basic philosophy of teaching was straightforward and deeply personal. I wanted to teach the way I wished that I myself had been taught. Which is to say, I hoped to convey the sheer joy of learning, the thrill of understanding things about the universe. I wanted to pass along to students not only the logic but the beauty of math and science. Furthermore, I wanted to do this in a way that would be equally helpful to kids studying a subject for the first time and for adults who wanted to refresh their knowledge; for students grappling with homework and for older people hoping to keep their minds active and supple.

What I *didn't* want was the dreary process that sometimes went on in classrooms—rote memorization and plug-in formulas aimed at nothing more lasting or meaningful than a good grade on the next exam. Rather, I hoped to help students see the connections, the progression, between one lesson and the next; to hone their intuitions so that mere information, absorbed one concept at a time, could develop into true mastery of a subject. In a word, I wanted to restore the excitement—

the active participation in learning and the natural high that went with it—that conventional curricula sometimes seemed to bludgeon into submission.

In the earliest days of what would become the Academy, I had one student, Nadia. She happened to be my cousin.

By the middle of 2012, Khan Academy had grown well beyond me. We were helping to educate more than six million unique students per month—more than ten times the number of people who have gone to Harvard since its inception in 1636—and this number was growing by 400 percent per year. The videos had been viewed over 140 million times and students had done nearly half a billion exercises through our software. I had personally posted more than three thousand video lessons—all free, untainted by commercials—covering everything from basic arithmetic to advanced calculus, from physics to finance to biology, from chemistry to the French Revolution. We were also aggressively hiring the best educators and software engineers in the world to help. The Academy had become the most used education platform on the Web, described by *Forbes* as "one of those why-didn't-anyone-think-of-that stories ... [that] is rapidly becoming the most influential teaching organization on the planet." Bill Gates had paid the high compliment of publicly acknowledging that he used the site while working on math problems with his own kids.

This book, in part, is the story of the astonishing acceptance and growth of khanacademy.org—and, more important, what that growth tells us about the world we live in.

A few short years ago, Khan Academy was known only to a handful of middle-school kids—relatives and family friends. How and why, from those intimate beginnings, did awareness of the site spread to a worldwide community of people of all ages and economic conditions who were hungry to learn? Why did students tell their friends and, eventually, their teachers? Why did teachers pass the word to their department heads? Why did parents adopt the site not only as a way to help their children, but also to refresh their own memories and appetite to learn?

In short, what unmet needs was the Academy fulfilling?

Why was the Academy managing to motivate and excite students in ways that conventional curricula had failed to do? As to results, could we demonstrate, with real data, that the Academy was helping people learn? Did it boost test scores? Even more important, did the Academy's way of teaching help people retain real understanding for longer? Did it consistently help students move beyond their grade level in school? Were the video lessons and interactive software most useful as an add-on to the conventional classroom, or were they pointing the way to a fundamentally different future for education—above all, an *active and self-paced* future?

For each individual student, age eight or eighty, the next video would always be a personal discovery. The next set of problems and exercises would constitute a challenge that each person could approach at his or her own tempo; there would be no shame or stigma in progressing slowly, no dreaded moment when *the class must move on*. The archive of videos would never go away; students could review and refresh as often as necessary. And mistakes would be allowed! There'd be no fear of disappointing a teacher who is looking over one's shoulder, of appearing dumb in front of a roomful of peers.

I passionately believe that the Khan Academy is a tool that can empower at least an approximate model of what the future of education should look like—a way of combining the art of teaching with the science of presenting information and analyzing data, of delivering the clearest, most comprehensive, and most relevant curriculum at the lowest possible cost. I have many reasons for believing this, some to do with technology, some with economics. But perhaps the most compelling is the feedback we have heard from students.

Over the past few years, we have received thousands of email testimonials from students who have benefited from the Academy. These messages have come from European cities, from American suburbs, from villages in India, from towns in the Middle East where young women, sometimes in secret, are trying to get an education. Some of these emails have been brief and funny; others have been detailed and heartfelt, sometimes from kids who'd been struggling in school and feeling bad about themselves, sometimes from adults who'd feared they'd lost the capacity to learn.

From all these many messages, certain themes have clearly emerged. Far too many bright, motivated kids are being badly served by their educational experiences—ones at elite, wealthy schools as well as underfunded ones. Too many kids are having their confidence trampled; even many "successful" students acknowledge that they've gotten good grades without learning much of anything. Kids and adults alike are having their curiosity drained away by boredom in class or the workplace, and by the unremitting background noise of a dumbed-down pop culture.

For these students, the Khan Academy has been a haven and a refuge, a place where they can do for themselves what their classroom and workplace experiences have failed to do. Can watching video lessons or using interactive software make people smart? No. But I would argue that it can do something even better: create a context in which people can give free rein to their curiosity and natural love of learning, so that they realize they're *already* smart.

More than anything, it is the student testimonials that have persuaded me to write this book. I think of it as a kind of manifesto—both a very personal statement and a call to arms. Formal education must change. It needs to be brought into closer alignment *with the world as it actually is*; into closer harmony with the way human beings actually learn and thrive.

When and where do people concentrate best? The answer, of course, is that it all depends on the individual. Some people are at their sharpest first thing in the morning. Some are more receptive late at night. One person requires a silent house to optimize his focus; another seems to think more clearly with music playing or against the white noise of a coffee shop. Given all these variations, why do we still insist that the heaviest lifting in teaching and learning should take place in the confines of a classroom and to the impersonal rhythm of bells and buzzers?

Technology has the power to free us from those limitations,

to make education far more portable, flexible, and personal; to foster initiative and individual responsibility; to restore the treasure-hunt excitement to the process of learning. Technology offers another potential benefit as well: The Internet can make education far, far more accessible, so knowledge and opportunity can be more broadly and equitably shared. Quality education need not be dependent on showplace campuses. There is no economic reason that students everywhere could not have access to the same lessons as Bill Gates's kids.

There's an old saying that *life is school*. If that's true, then it's also true that as our world grows smaller and the people in it more inextricably connected, the world itself comes to resemble one vast, inclusive schoolhouse. There are younger people and older people, people farther or less far along in their education on a given subject. At every moment, we are both students and teachers; we learn by studying, but we also learn by helping others, by sharing and explaining what we know.

I like to think of Khan Academy as a virtual extension of this One World Schoolhouse. It's a place where all are welcome, all are invited to teach as well as learn, and all are encouraged to do the best they can. Success is self-defined; the only failure lies in giving up. Speaking for myself, I have learned as much from the Academy as I have taught. I have gotten back—in intellectual pleasure, refreshed curiosity, and a sense of connection to other minds and other people—more than I have put in. It's my hope that every Academy student and every reader of this book will be able to say the same.

PART 1

Learning to Teach

Teaching Nadia

There is an art, or rather, a knack to flying. The knack lies in learning how to throw yourself at the ground and miss. Pick a nice day and try it.

—DOUGLAS ADAMS, THE HITCHHIKER'S
GUIDE TO THE GALAXY

This story starts with one student and one teacher. It begins as a family story, so let me tell you a bit about my background.

I was born in Metairie, Louisiana, a residential area within metro New Orleans. My father, a pediatrician, had moved there from Bangladesh for his medical residency at LSU and, later, his practice at Charity Hospital. In 1972, he briefly returned to Bangladesh and came back with my mother—who was born in India. It was an arranged marriage, very traditional (my mother tried to peek during the ceremony to make sure she was marrying the brother she thought she was). Over the next several years, five of my mother's brothers and one cousin came to visit, and they all fell in love with the New Orleans area. I believe that they did this because Louisiana was as close to South Asia as the United States could get; it had spicy food, humidity, giant cockroaches, and a corrupt government. We were a close family—even though, at any given moment, half of my relatives weren't speaking to the other half.

Still, a family wedding was a big occasion, so when I got married in 2004, more than forty relatives made the long trip to New Jersey, where my wife's family lived. One of them was my cousin Nadia.

Today, Nadia is a pre-med junior at Sarah Lawrence College. But in 2004 she was a very serious-minded twelve-year-old who had just had the first academic setback of her life. She'd done poorly on a math placement exam given at the end of sixth grade. She was a straight-A student, highly motivated, always prepared. Her subpar performance baffled her. It wounded her pride, her confidence, and her self-esteem.

By the time we spoke after my wedding, Nadia had actually come to accept the outcome of that test. She believed that she just wasn't good at math. I saw it very differently. I saw real potential in her. She was logical, creative, and tenacious. I was already viewing her as a future computer scientist or mathematician. It seemed inconceivable to me that she, of all people, would find something in the sixth grade difficult.

Having gone through the traditional academic system, it was also clear to me that being placed in the slower math class could be the kiss of death for her mathematical future. Because of "tracking"—a subject we'll have occasion to come back to—this one test result would have huge ramifications for Nadia's academic destiny. If she didn't get into the more advanced track, she wouldn't be able to take algebra in eighth grade. If she didn't take algebra in eighth grade, she wouldn't be able to take calculus in twelfth. And so on, down a slippery slope that would leave her far short of her potential.

But a botched test was a botched test. Was there anything to be done about it? Nadia's mother didn't think so, and during a post-wedding visit to Boston, where I lived and worked, it became clear that she was very distressed. So I made a somewhat rash offer. If Nadia's school would let her retake the exam, I would tutor her, remotely, when she was back in New Orleans. As to exactly *how* I would tutor her...well, that was a work in progress.

Let me be clear—I think it's essential for everything that follows—that at the start this was all an experiment, an improvisation. I'd had no teacher training, no Big Idea for the most effective way to teach. I did feel that I understood math intuitively and holistically, but this was no guarantee that I'd be effective as a teacher. I'd had plenty of professors who knew their subject cold but simply weren't very good at sharing what they knew. I believed, and still believe, that teaching is a separate skill—in fact, an art that is creative, intuitive, and highly personal.

But it isn't *only* an art. It has, or should have, some of the rigor of science as well. I felt that I could experiment with different techniques to see what worked and what didn't, that with time I could develop myself into an effective tutor for Nadia. It was an intellectual challenge not too different from those I faced in the investing or technology worlds, but this one had the very real potential to empower someone I cared about.

I had no preconceived notions about how people learned;

I was constrained by no orthodoxy regarding the "right" way to do things. I was feeling my way for how best to convey information and to employ the available technology. In short, I was starting from square one, without habits or assumptions. It's not just that I was thinking outside the box; for me, there was no box. I tried things and I saw what worked. By extension, I also inferred what *hadn't* been working.

Actually, I did bring a few assumptions into my approach to working with Nadia, though they were based on personal experience rather than on any sort of pedagogic theory. During my own school years I'd felt that some teachers were more interested in showing off what they knew than in communicating it to me. Their tone was often impatient, occasionally arrogant and even condescending. Other teachers were scripted to the point that it didn't feel like they were actually even thinking. I wanted our tutorial sessions to be a safe, personal, comfortable, thought-provoking experience. I wanted to be a tutor who genuinely shared his thinking and expressed it in a conversational style, as if I was speaking to an equal who was fundamentally smart but just didn't fully understand the material at hand.

I firmly believed that Nadia, and most people, could understand the math. I didn't want her to memorize and I certainly didn't want her to compartmentalize. I was convinced that if she understood the conceptual underpinnings of mathematics, the flow of one idea to the next, everything else would be easy.

In any case, the first step in tutoring Nadia was to figure out what aspect of the math test had given her trouble. It turned out that she had stumbled on the concept of unit conversion. This surprised me. Unit conversion—figuring out how many feet in six miles, or how many ounces in three pints, and so forth—was a fairly straightforward notion. You learned a few terms—*kilo* for a thousand, *centi* for a hundredth—and the rest of the factors you could easily look up. From there it was a simple matter of multiplication or division. Nadia had done just fine with far subtler concepts in math.

So why did she have trouble with unit conversion? She didn't know, and neither did I. But let's think about a few of the possible reasons that she might not have "gotten" this particular topic.

Maybe she was absent on the day it was introduced in class. Maybe she was physically present but not at her best. Maybe she was sleepy, or had a bellyache, or was upset about an argument with her mom. Maybe she had an exam in the class that came next, and was cramming for that instead of paying attention. Maybe she had a crush on a boy two rows over and was daydreaming about him. Maybe her teacher was in a hurry to move on and just didn't explain it very well.

These are only conjectures; the point is that there are any number of things that *might* have prevented Nadia from catching on to unit conversion, and that once the concept had passed her by, *it wasn't coming back in class.* That module had been covered. Those problems had been worked on and erased. There was a curriculum to follow, a schedule to keep; *the class had to move on.*

Let's take a moment to consider this. It so happened that Nadia attended a fine prep school, with an excellent student/ teacher ratio and quite small class sizes. Class size, of course, is an obsession among those who believe that our standard educational model would work just fine if only we could afford more teachers, more buildings, more textbooks, more computers—more of everything except students, so that class sizes could be reduced (essentially making poor schools look more like rich ones). Now, no one is *against* the idea of smaller classes; I want as low of a ratio as economically possible for my own children so they have time to really form bonds with their teachers. Unfortunately, however, the idea that smaller classes alone will magically solve the problem of students being left behind is a fallacy.

It ignores several basic facts about how people actually learn. People learn at different rates. Some people seem to catch on to things in quick bursts of intuition; others grunt and grind their way toward comprehension. Quicker isn't necessarily smarter and slower definitely isn't dumber. Further, catching on quickly isn't the same as understanding thoroughly. So the pace of learning is a question of style, not relative intelligence. The tortoise may very well end up with more knowledge—more useful, *lasting* knowledge—than the hare.

Moreover, a student who is slow at learning arithmetic may be off the charts when it comes to the abstract creativity needed in higher mathematics. The point is that whether there are ten or twenty or fifty kids in a class, there will be disparities in their grasp of a topic at any given time. Even a one-to-one ratio is not ideal if the teacher feels forced to march the student along at a state-mandated pace, regardless of how well the concepts are understood. When that rather arbitrary "snapshot" moment comes along—when it's time to wrap up the module, give the exam, and move on—there will still likely be some students who haven't quite figured things out.

They could probably figure things out *eventually*—but that's exactly the problem. The standard classroom model doesn't really allow for *eventual* understanding. The class—of whatever size—has moved on.

In muddling toward my own approach to tutoring, then— in trying to match my methods to how I thought people really learn—two of my first precepts were these: that lessons should be paced to the individual student's needs, not to some arbitrary calendar; and that basic concepts needed to be deeply understood if students were to succeed at mastering more advanced ones.

But let's come back to Nadia.

She returned to school in New Orleans. I resumed my working life in Boston. I'd equipped us both with inexpensive pen tablets that would allow us to see each other's scrawls on our respective computers, using a program called Yahoo Doodle. We scheduled sessions to talk on the phone and figure out this troublesome business of unit conversion.

The first week of tutoring was pure torture—torture for me, and I'm guessing it was ten times worse for her. But it taught me, in a very immediate and intimate manner, about some of the many complicating factors that get in the way of learning.

There was no doubt that Nadia was extremely bright. When she and her family had visited me in Boston, we'd killed some time by working on a battery of brain teasers while waiting for the Fourth of July fireworks to start over the Charles River. What I most remembered was how willing Nadia was to tackle hard problems. How analytical and creative she was. How she was able to logically break down questions that I've seen interviewees from top engineering and business schools struggle with. Yet when it came to unit conversion, her brain just seemed to shut down. It froze; it locked. Why? It seemed to me that she'd just plain psyched herself out. Like many people who'd had difficulty with a particular subject, she'd told herself she'd never get it, and that was that.

I told her, "Nadia, you've mastered much harder things than this. You'll get this, too."

Either she didn't hear me or she thought I was lying to her. We started doing problems. I'd ask a question. There'd be a silence—a silence that went on so long I sometimes thought we'd lost the telephone or Internet connection. Finally her answer would come, meekly, with her voice turning up at the end. "A thousand?"

"Nadia, are you guessing?"

"A hundred?"

I was starting to get seriously concerned that perhaps I was doing Nadia more harm than good. With nothing but kind intentions, I was causing her a lot of discomfort and anxiety. My hope had been to restore her confidence; maybe I was damaging it still further.

This forced me to acknowledge that sometimes the presence of a teacher—either in the room or at the other end of a telephone connection; either in a class of thirty or tutoring one-to-one—can be a source of student thought-paralysis. From the teacher's perspective, what's going on is a helping relationship; but from the student's point of view, it's difficult if not impossible to avoid an element of confrontation. A question is asked; an answer is expected *immediately*; that brings pressure. The student doesn't want to disappoint the teacher. She fears she will be judged. And all these factors interfere with the student's ability to fully concentrate on the matter at hand. Even more, students are embarrassed to communicate what they do and do not understand.

With that in mind—and partly out of sheer exasperation—I tried a somewhat different strategy. I said, "Nadia, I know you're smart. I'm not judging you. But we're changing the rules here. You're not allowed to guess, and you're not allowed to give me wishy-washy answers. There are only two things I want to hear. Either give me a definite, confident answer—yell it out!—or say, 'Sal, I don't understand. Please go over it again.' You don't have to get it the first time. I won't think less of you for asking questions or wanting something repeated. Okay?" I think it might have pissed her off a bit, but it had the right effect. She began decisively, and somewhat angrily, to shout answers—or admissions of lack of understanding—back at me.

Very soon after that, Nadia seemed to have one of those *Aha* moments. Unit conversion rather suddenly started making sense and the tutoring sessions became a lot of fun. Which came first, the success or the enjoyment? I don't really know, and I don't think it matters. What does matter is that along with her growing comfort with the subject, Nadia's confidence and alertness came roaring back. I could hear her pleasure when she knew an answer. More important, there was no embarrassment or shame when she needed something explained again—when she hit the replay button, so to speak.

There was also another aspect to Nadia's changed mood.

Once she started understanding unit conversion, she was angry that she hadn't gotten it before. It was a healthy, useful kind of anger. She was mad at herself for feeling daunted, for doubting her own abilities, for having given in to discouragement. Now that she'd conquered one recalcitrant subject, she'd be much less likely to let herself be daunted ever again.

Nadia went on to retake her math exam, and passed with flying colors. In the meantime, I had also started tutoring her younger brothers, Arman and Ali. Word got out to a few other family members and friends, and before long I had around ten students. Though I didn't realize it at the time, the Khan Academy was mysteriously coming into being—was being *pulled* into being by the curiosity and needs of its students and their families. The invisible process of its going somewhat viral was already in the first tiny stage of gathering momentum.

All of my tutees, I'm proud to say, were soon doing work way beyond their grade levels—and I was hooked on teaching. I couldn't help comparing the substance and satisfaction of my tutoring work to the money-based routines of my day job at the hedge fund. Now, I definitely don't agree with the knee-jerk opinion that hedge funds are evil; the majority of the people in the field are actually highly intellectual, good people. Still, the focus of a workday in investing is not exactly social service. Was that really how I wanted to spend my life? Was that really the best use of my limited time on Earth?

I was in a bind. I was stuck in a job I really liked—it was challenging and intellectually and financially rewarding. But I had a nagging feeling that I was being held back from a calling I saw as far more worthwhile.

So I kept the day job and saved my pennies, looking forward to the time when I could afford to quit. In the meantime, I started experimenting with various techniques that might make me more efficient in serving my growing roster of tutees; again, I took a problem-solving, nuts-and-bolts approach to this—an engineer's approach.

I tried to schedule Skype sessions with three or four students at a time. The logistics were unwieldy, and the lessons themselves not as effective as working one-to-one. To help automate things, I wrote some software that would generate questions and keep track of how each student did with the responses. I enjoyed writing the program, and it did give me valuable insights into where I should focus the time during the live sessions. As we will see later in our story, these techniques for gathering, organizing, and interpreting data have by now become useful and sophisticated tools. The software by itself, however, didn't solve the problem of making the live sessions more scalable.

Then, just when I was starting to feel that I'd taken on too much and should probably back away, a friend came up with a suggestion: Why didn't I record the lessons and post them on YouTube, so that each student could watch them at his or her convenience?

At once, I saw that the idea was...ridiculous! YouTube? YouTube was for cats playing the piano, not serious mathematics. A serious, systematic curriculum on *YouTube*? Clearly, a harebrained notion.

Some three thousand videos later, I still wish I'd thought of it myself.

No-Frills Videos

In character, in manner, in style, in all things, the supreme excellence is simplicity.
—Henry Wadsworth Longfellow

To those who believe that quality education requires showplace campuses and state-of-the-art classrooms, and is therefore a luxury item available only to wealthy communities in wealthy countries, I'd like to point out a few things about the early days of the Academy. For example, our headquarters was first a guest bedroom and then, more famously, a closet. True, it was a walk-in closet, with electrical outlets, room for a small desk, and even a window overlooking the garden. But it was a closet nonetheless. I thought of it as a kind of monk's cell, a place to concentrate without distractions or the temptations of too much comfort.

In the formative years of the Academy, I was still muddling my way toward the most effective methods for presenting the video lessons. I was guided in part by my own taste and temperament, which tended toward the austere.

Early on, for example, I decided that I wanted the background of my computer "chalkboard" to be black. Even though it was now virtual, I felt that there was something magical about a blackboard. One of my key hopes was to remind students of the excitement of learning, to bring back the fun and even the suspense that ensued when the quest for understanding was seen as a kind of treasure hunt. What better way, graphically, to suggest this than by showing problems and solutions seeming to emerge from the void? Knowledge brought light out of darkness. With application and focus, students found answers where before there had been nothing but a blank.

Another formative and crucial decision had to do with the duration of the lessons. Back when I was tutoring Nadia over the phone, we had no particular time constraints. We talked until one or the other of us had to go, or until a certain concept had been covered, or until a certain level of frustration or mental fatigue had been reached; the length of our sessions was not determined by the clock. But when I started posting videos on YouTube, I had to abide by their guidelines. Although their rules have now changed for certain kinds of content, there was then a ten-minute limit for what the site would post. So my lessons were just about ten minutes long.

And it turned out that ten minutes, give or take, was the right length for them to be.

Let me make it clear that I did not *discover* this fact. I stumbled upon it by a mix of intuition and serendipity. But the truth is that well-credentialed educational theorists had long before determined that ten to eighteen minutes was about the limit of students' attention spans.

Back in 1996, in *National Teaching & Learning Forum*, two professors from Indiana University, Joan Middendorf and Alan Kalish, published an account of the ebbs and flows of students' focus during a typical class period. It should be noted that this report centered on college students, and of course it was done before the age of texting and tweeting; presumably, the attention spans of younger people today have become even shorter, or certainly more challenged by distractions.

In any case, breaking the session down minute by minute, the professors determined that students needed a three- to five-minute period of settling down, which would be followed by ten to eighteen minutes of optimal focus. Then—no matter how good the teacher or how compelling the subject matter—there would come a lapse. In the vernacular, the kids would "lose it." Attention would eventually return, but in ever briefer packets, falling "to three or four minutes towards the end of a standard lecture."[1]

An even earlier study, from 1985, had tested students on their recall of facts contained in a twenty-minute presentation. For purposes of scoring, the researcher broke the presentation into four segments of five minutes each. While you might expect that recall would be greatest regarding the final section of the presentation—the part heard most recently—in fact the result was strikingly opposite. Students remembered far more of what they'd heard at the very beginning of the lecture. By the fifteen-minute mark, they'd mostly zoned out.[2]

My point here is that long before Khan Academy or YouTube even existed, solid academic research had gone a long way toward describing the length and shape and limits of students' attention spans. Yet these findings—which were quite dramatic, consistent, and conclusive, and have never yet been refuted—went largely unapplied in the real world.

Curiously, in the Middendorf and Kalish study, even the researchers themselves shrank from applying their own conclusions. Having established that students' attention maxed out at around ten or fifteen minutes, they still regarded it as a given that classroom sessions lasted an hour. They suggested, therefore, that teachers insert "change-ups" at various points in their lectures, "to restart the attention clock." Perhaps, in the hands of skilled and resourceful teachers, these "change-ups" were effective in refreshing kids' focus. Still, there was something gimmicky and beside the point about the whole idea; it went directly against the grain of the findings. If attention lasted ten or fifteen minutes, why did it remain a given that class periods were an hour?

Or again, if the "change-ups"—things like small-group discussions or active problem-solving—recharged student focus, why was the broadcast lecture still the dominant mode? Why was it still presumed that students would spend most of their day passively listening?

The bottom line is that the research—and, frankly, experience and common sense—pointed in a certain clear direction, but there was too much inertia to the already existing model to do anything about it.

Now, there are some exceptions. Many college courses in the humanities focus on discussion over lecture. Students read course material ahead of time and have a discussion in class. Harvard Business School took this to the extreme by pioneering case-based learning more than a hundred years ago, and many business schools have since followed suit. There are no lectures there, not even in subjects like accounting or finance. Students read a ten- to twenty-page description of a particular company's or person's circumstance—called a "case"—on their own time and then participate in a discussion/debate in class (where attendance is mandatory). Professors are there to facilitate the discussion, not to dominate it. I can tell you from personal experience that despite there being eighty students in the room, you cannot zone out. Your brain is actively processing what your peers are saying while you try to come to your own conclusions so that you can contribute during the entire eighty-minute session. The time goes by faster than you want it to; students are more engaged than in any traditional classroom I've ever been a part of.

Most importantly, the ideas that you and your peers collectively generate *stick*. To this day, comments and ways of thinking about a problem that my peers shared with me (or that I shared during class) nearly ten years ago come back to me as I try to help manage the growth and opportunities surrounding the Khan Academy.

Focusing on the Content

Art is the elimination of the unnecessary.
—PABLO PICASSO

The duration of the YouTube lessons is hardly the only instance in which Khan Academy teaching methods—arrived at largely by serendipity and intuition—turned out to be neither more nor less than the implementation of sound pedagogic research that had been accepted in theory but never really been applied. As we'll see, this is a recurring theme.

For right now, however, I'd like to introduce another factor that was a key consideration in shaping my approach to teaching: cost. I was bankrolling the Academy solely from my personal savings. I loved teaching, but I didn't want to go broke doing it. When it came to posting the video lessons, I wanted to keep the equipment and production costs to an absolute minimum.

It was partly for this reason—and not because of some pre-existing theory—that I decided that I would never be pictured in the lessons. I didn't at the time own a suitable video camera, and I didn't want to buy one. It seemed like a slippery slope. If I had a camera, I would have to worry about the lighting. If I had good lighting, I would have to give thought to what I was wearing and whether I had spinach in my teeth. The danger was that the whole process would become more like making movies than tutoring students. Tutoring is intimate. You talk *with* someone, not *at* someone. I wanted students to feel like they were sitting next to me at the kitchen table, elbow to elbow, working out problems together. I didn't want to appear as a talking head at a blackboard, lecturing from across the room. So it was determined that students would never see me but only hear my voice, while the visuals would be nothing except my scrawls (and occasional historic images) on the black electronic chalkboard. Students would see the same thing I was seeing.

Human beings are also hardwired to focus on faces. We are constantly scanning the facial expressions of those around us to get information about the emotional state of the room and our place in it. We seem to be hardwired to meet each other's gazes, to read lips even as we are listening. Anyone who has ever raised a baby has noticed its particular attention while looking at its mother; indeed, its parents' faces are probably the very first things a newborn manages to focus on.

So if faces are so important to human beings, why exclude them from videos? Because they are a powerful distraction from the concepts being discussed. What, after all, is more distracting than a pair of blinking human eyes, a nose that twitches, and a mouth that moves with every word? Put a face in the same frame as an equation, and the eye will bounce back and forth between the two. Concentration will wander.

Haven't we all had the experience of losing the thread of a conversation because we homed in on the features of the person we were talking with rather than paying steady attention to what was being said?

This is not to say that faces—both the teacher's and the student's—are unimportant to the teaching process. On the contrary, face time shared by teachers and students is one of the things that humanizes the classroom experience, that lets both teachers and students shine in their uniqueness. Through facial expressions, teachers convey empathy, approval, and all the many nuances of concern. Students, in turn, reveal their stresses and uncertainties, as well as their pleasure when a concept finally becomes clear.

But for all of that, the face time can and should be *a separate thing* from first exposure to concepts. And these two aspects of the educational experience, far from being in conflict, should complement one another. The computer-based lessons free up valuable class time that would otherwise be spent on broadcast lectures—a model in which the students generally sit blankly with no effective way for teachers to appraise who's "getting it" and who is not. By contrast, if the students have done the lessons *before* the interaction, then there's actually something to talk about. There are opportunities for interchange. This last point needs to be emphasized, because some people fear that computer-based instruction is all about replacing teachers or lowering the level of skill needed to be a teacher. The exact opposite is true. Teachers become more important once students have the initial exposure to a concept online (either through videos or exercises). Teachers can then carve out face time with individual students who are struggling; they can move away from rote lecturing and into the higher tasks of mentoring, inspiring, and providing perspective.

This suggests something that is at the very heart of my belief system: that when it comes to education, technology is not to be feared, but embraced; used wisely and sensitively, computer-based lessons actually allow teachers to do more teaching, and the classroom to become a workshop for mutual helping, rather than passive sitting.

Mastery Learning

The nature of an innovation is that it will arise at a fringe where it can afford to become prevalent enough to establish its usefulness without being overwhelmed by the inertia of the orthodox system.

—KEVIN KELLY, COFOUNDER OF *WIRED* MAGAZINE

Before moving on from this brief introduction of some of the bedrock principles and intuitions upon which the Academy's methods were founded, I'd like to mention one other important concept that will figure significantly in our story: *mastery learning.*

At its most fundamental, mastery learning simply suggests that students should adequately comprehend a given concept before being expected to understand a more advanced one. While this seems straightforward and commonsensical enough, mastery learning has had a rocky and controversial history that is of interest for at least two reasons. First, it constitutes another instance of the education establishment failing to follow up on its own best research and soundest advice. Second, because of advances in technology, it is finally possible—nearly a century after the advantages of mastery learning were first described and tested—to broadly apply its methods and techniques to real schools and real students.

Here's a little history. Way back in 1919—before there were computers, or television, or antibiotics—a progressive educator named Carleton W. Washburne was named superintendent of schools in the affluent Chicago suburb of Winnetka, Illinois. The time and place were right for innovation. The victory in World War I had boosted national morale and helped create the American can-do spirit. Economic times were on the upswing; Winnetka was a manageably sized school system with the will and the means to experiment and excel. In 1922, Washburne introduced what became widely known as the Winnetka Plan.

At its heart was the somewhat radical concept of mastery learning. What made mastery learning radical? Two things. First, it was predicated on the belief that *all* students could learn if provided with conditions appropriate to their needs; no one should have to be "held back" or put on a track that leads to academic failure.

Second, mastery learning structured its curriculum not in terms of *time*, but in terms of certain target levels of comprehension and achievement. This turned tradition quietly but entirely upside down. In the traditional model, a certain amount of class time is devoted to a particular topic or concept; when the allotted interval is finished, the entire class moves on, in spite of the fact that individual students will have achieved widely varying degrees of mastery over the material. In Washburne's system, by contrast, students, with the help of self-paced exercises, proceed at varying rates toward *the same level* of mastery. Those who learn more quickly can move ahead or do "enrichment exercises." Those who learn more slowly are helped along by individual tutoring, or peer assistance, or additional homework.

Let me emphasize this difference, because it is central to everything I argue for in this book. In a traditional academic model, the time allotted to learn something is fixed while the comprehension of the concept is variable. Washburne was advocating the opposite. What should be fixed is a high level of comprehension and what should be variable is the amount of time students have to understand a concept.

During the progressive 1920s, interest in the Winnetka Plan ran high. Self-instruction "workbooks" were in demand around the country. Carleton Washburne himself became an academic star, going on to serve as president of the Progressive Education Association and to join the faculty of Brooklyn College. But then a strange thing happened to the notion of mastery learning. It soon went out of vogue, and for years—for decades—it was all but forgotten.

Why? Part of the reason, no doubt, was economic. A small, wealthy school system like Winnetka's could afford the new textbooks and exercise tablets and other materials required by the system; but the technology of paper publishing was expensive, and probably impractical on a nationwide scale. Then, too, there was the issue of teacher retraining; mastery learning did in fact call for a somewhat different set of techniques and skills, which in turn called not only for money but for initiative and flexibility on the part of teachers and administrators.

Largely, though, what killed mastery learning, 1920s style, seems to have been simple inertia and resistance to new and threatening ideas. In a truly shocking 1989 study, it was concluded that between 1893 and 1979, "instructional practice [in public schools] remained about the same" (and it really hasn't changed from 1979 to 2012 either)![3] To be sure, some very innovative groups of teachers and schools have been experimenting with new techniques within their classrooms, but the mainstream model did not change in any appreciable way. Did no one notice how much the world was changing, and how much the educational needs of students were evolving as well?

In any case, the concept of mastery learning seems to have been smothered under the vast weight of educational orthodoxy, and it languished until the next progressive era—the 1960s—when it was revived, in slightly different form, by a developmental psychologist named Benjamin Bloom and his leading protégé, James Block.[4] Bloom and Block suggested refinements in testing methods and the delivery of feedback, but their basic principles came straight out of the Winnetka Plan. Students learned at their own pace, advancing to the next concept only after reaching a prescribed degree of mastery over the previous concept. Teachers served primarily as guides and mentors rather than lecturers. Peer interaction was encouraged; peers helping peers was of benefit not only academically, but in character-building as well. Some students might struggle, but none were given up on.

Mastery learning techniques were soon being applied in various pilot programs around the country. In study after study, mastery learning kicked butt when compared to conventional classroom models.

One research paper concluded that "students in mastery learning programs at all levels showed increased gains in achievement over those in traditional instruction programs.... Students retained what they had learned longer under mastery learning, both in short-term and long-term studies."[5] Another study found that "mastery learning reduces the academic spread between the slower and faster students without slowing down the faster students."[6] Shifting the emphasis from students to teachers, yet another study recorded that "teachers who [used] mastery learning...began to feel better about teaching and their roles as teachers."[7]

Well, with reviews like that, you might have thought that mastery learning would be a long-running show. But it wasn't. As in the 1920s, the method enjoyed a brief vogue, then was swamped by the stagnant waters of traditional classroom procedures. As before, the reason was partly economic; it still cost money to print and distribute all those workbooks, test forms, and individualized reading materials. But money wasn't the only hurdle. Once again there was the resistance of administrators and bureaucrats. Change was difficult; change was frightening. The old way worked well enough...didn't it? Lacking some clear and present urgency to leave the comfort zone of lectures and traditional textbooks, why bother? And so in spite of the fact that mastery learning had consistently demonstrated both anecdotal and statistical benefits for both students and teachers, it went out of fashion once again.

Cut to the present moment. Human nature hasn't changed.

Bureaucrats and organizations still seem to have a built-in aversion to new ideas and approaches. People in all fields still have a tendency to protect their turf, sometimes at the expense of the greater good. In other regards, however, things are quite different this time around. More than ever before, there *is* a sense of urgency when it comes to educational reform. The old system is failing us; it needs to be rethought. On this there is broad agreement.

The other thing that has changed—and this is huge—is that technology has radically lowered the expenses formerly associated with mastery learning. No more paper workbooks. No more pricey printings of individualized exercises. Everything needed for self-paced learning is right there in the computer; the cost of delivering it to students is miniscule. The old excuse that newfangled teaching methods are just too expensive—or are only the province of elite schools in privileged communities—just no longer applies.

There's one more aspect of mastery learning systems that I'd like to explore before moving on: the relationship between mastery learning and personal responsibility.

Taking responsibility for education—responsibility on the part of students, families, communities, and nations—is of course a hot-button issue these days, approached and argued from all points on the political compass. Too often, however, the suggestion is made that "taking responsibility" is somehow an independent thing from the learning itself, and that responsibility can be put on the shoulders of parents and teachers without necessarily involving the student. Both of those notions are false. Taking responsibility for education *is* education; taking responsibility for learning *is* learning. From the student's perspective, only by taking responsibility does true learning become possible; studies of mastery learning dynamics make this clear.

In one such study, it was observed that students in mastery programs "developed more positive attitudes about learning and about their ability to learn."[8] To use a contemporary expression, they were more likely to claim ownership of their educations. Another study concluded simply that "students who learned under mastery conditions...accepted greater responsibility for their learning."[9]

I stress this because I believe that *personal responsibility* is not only undervalued but actually discouraged by the standard classroom model, with its enforced passivity and rigid boundaries of curriculum and time. Denied the opportunity to make even the most basic decisions about how and what they will learn, students stop short of full commitment.

Mastery learning, then, is another one of those ideas for which I take no credit whatsoever. Both the concept itself and the data in support of its effectiveness have been around for quite a while. But as we'll see in due course, the Khan Academy presents an opportunity to apply its principles and reap its benefits far more broadly than ever before.

How Education Happens

Learning without thought is labor lost; thought without learning is perilous.

—Confucius

Let's consider an incredibly fundamental riddle: How does education happen?

I see it as an extremely active, even athletic process. Teachers can convey information. They can assist and they can inspire—and these are important and beautiful things. At the end of the day, however, the fact is that *we educate ourselves*. We learn, first of all, by deciding to learn, by committing to learning. This commitment allows, in turn, for concentration. Concentration pertains not only to the immediate task at hand but to all the many associations that surround it. All of these processes are active and deeply personal; all involve the acceptance of responsibility. Education doesn't happen out in the ether, and it doesn't happen in the empty space between the teacher's lips and the students' ears; it happens in the individual brains of each of us.

This is no mere metaphor, but a physical reality. The Nobel Prize–winning neuroscientist Eric R. Kandel, in his seminal book *In Search of Memory*, argues that learning is in fact neither more nor less than a series of changes that take place in the individual nerve cells of which our brains are composed. When a given cell is involved in learning, it literally *grows*. The process is not exactly analogous to what happens when one exercises a muscle, but it's pretty close. Without getting too terribly technical, what happens is that an "educated" neuron actually develops new synaptic terminals—these being the tiny appendages across which one neuron communicates with the next. The increase in the number of active terminals makes the nerve cell more efficient in passing messages along. As this process is repeated along an entire neural pathway leading to a particular region of the brain, the information is gathered and stored. As we work with the same concept from slightly different angles and investigate questions surrounding it, we build even more and deeper connections. Collectively, this web of connections and associations comprises what we think of informally as *understanding*.

In physiological terms, then, learning means that our brains have done some exercise—digested information, connected concepts and memories in new ways—and our nerve cells have thereby been altered.

How durable will this new understanding be? That depends, in part, on how actively the learning was acquired in the first place. Again, learning involves *physical* changes in the brain. Proteins are synthesized; synapses are enhanced. There's a lot of chemical and electrical work going on, and this is why thinking actually burns a lot of calories. The more neurons recruited into the learning process, the more vivid and lasting the memory. These physical changes in the brain, however, are not permanent. What we think of as "forgetting" is actually the gradual loss or weakening of the extra connections acquired in the process of learning. But there's good news here as well. As Kandel and other researchers have noticed, we don't lose *all* the extra synapses we've acquired. Again, an analogy with physical exercise, while inexact, is helpful; stop working out for a while and you will lose some but not all of the strength you had acquired. Some of the benefit will remain.

This is why it's easier to learn something a second time; at least some of the necessary neural pathways are already there. It's also a good incentive to bear down and concentrate the first time around, to etch the connections as durably as possible.

The findings of Kandel and other neuroscientists have much to say about how we actually learn; unfortunately, the standard classroom model tends to ignore or even to fly in the face of these fundamental biological truths. Stressing passivity over activity is one such misstep. Another, equally important, is the failure of standard education to maximize the brain's capacity for *associative learning*—the achieving of deeper comprehension and more durable memory by relating something newly learned to something already known. Let's take a moment to consider this.

Our brains hold two distinctly different kinds of memory—short-term and long-term. Short-term memory is not only fleeting, it's very fragile as well, easily disrupted by a lapse in concentration or by even a momentary detour into a different task or subject. (As an everyday example of this, I often forget if I have already used shampoo when I am in the shower.)

Long-term memory is far more stable and lasting, though of course not perfectly so. The process by which short-term memory becomes long-term memory is called *consolidation*. Brain scientists have yet to discover exactly how consolidation happens at the cellular level, but certain practical, functional characteristics of the process are well understood. As Kandel writes, "For a memory to persist, the incoming information must be thoroughly and deeply processed. This is accomplished by attending to the information and *associating it meaningfully and systematically with knowledge already well established in memory*" (italics mine).

In other words, it's easier to understand and remember something if we can relate it to something else we already know. This is why it's easier to memorize a poem than a series of nonsense syllables of equal length. In a poem, each word relates to images in our minds and to what has come before; there are rules of rhythm and connection that we understand, even if subliminally, the poem must follow. Rather than memorizing individual bits of information, we are dealing with patterns and strands of logic that allow us to come closer to seeing something whole.

This seems to be how our brains work best at retaining knowledge for the longer term, and it would certainly seem to suggest that the most effective way to teach would be to emphasize the *flow* of a subject, the chain of associations that relates one concept to the next and across subjects. Unfortunately, however, the standard approach to classroom teaching does just the opposite.

This is most obviously seen in the artificial separation

of traditional academic subjects. We lop them off at ultimately arbitrary places; we ghettoize them. Genetics is taught in biology while probability is taught in math, even though one is really an application of the other. Physics is a separate class from algebra and calculus despite its being a direct application of them. Chemistry is partitioned off from physics even though they study many of the same phenomena at different levels.

All of these divisions limit understanding and suggest a false picture of how the universe actually works. Wouldn't students find it useful to understand how contact forces (studied in physics) are in fact an expression of the repulsive forces between electrons (studied in chemistry)? Wouldn't algebra seem a tad more interesting if it could also be used to figure out how fast you hit the water on a belly flop or how heavy you would be on a planet twice Earth's mass? For that matter, think about the interesting cross-pollination that might occur if a value-neutral subject like computer science were studied together with a value-laden subject like evolution; what might students learn by writing computer programs to simulate variation and competition in an ecosystem?

The possibilities are endless, but they can't be realized given the balkanizing habits of our current system. Even within the already sawed-off classes, content is chunked into stand-alone episodes, and the connections are severed. In algebra, for example, students are taught to memorize the formula for the vertex of a parabola. Then they separately memorize the quadratic formula. In yet another lesson, they probably learn to "complete the square." The reality, however, is that all those formulas are expressions of essentially the same mathematical logic, so why aren't they taught together as the multiple facets of the same concept?

I'm not just nitpicking here. I believe that the breaking up of concepts like these has profound and even crucial consequences for how deeply students learn and how well they remember. It is the *connections* among concepts—or the lack of connections—that separate the students who memorize a formula for an exam only to forget it the next month and the students who internalize the concepts and are able to apply them when they need them a decade later.

This piecemeal approach to teaching is hardly limited to math and science. Similar instances can easily be found in the humanities. For an example from the subject of history, consider the Napoleonic Wars and the Louisiana Purchase. These were closely related events; Louisiana was offered at a fire-sale price only because Napoleon was desperate to finance his land wars in Europe and had had his navy destroyed at Trafalgar (so he couldn't protect Louisiana even if he wanted to keep it). But what are kids taught? If they're American, they tend to be taught that Thomas Jefferson got a great deal, with very little context as to why the Americans had a lot more negotiating leverage than Napoleon. These partial facts do nothing to promote an accurate understanding of how interconnected the world was and continues to be.

In our misplaced zeal for tidy categories and teaching modules that fit neatly into a given length of class time, we deny students the benefit—the physiological benefit—of recognizing connections. The conventional educational approach tends to be drearily consistent; take a *piece* of a subject and treat it as if it existed in a vacuum. Spend one or three or six weeks of classroom lectures on it, then give a test and move on. No wonder so many students acknowledge that they largely forget a subject soon after they've been tested on it.

Well, why *shouldn't* they forget? First of all, it's likely that they've been denied the mnemonic advantage of having this most recent module related to subjects that have come before or to their existing life experience. Second, chances are that the students have not been given a sufficient appreciation of how mastery of this topic will lead to a deeper understanding of things that come *after*. In short, if a given subject has been sealed, wrapped, and tied up with a bow—if the message is that the subject is *finished*—why bother to remember it?

In gradually developing my own approach to teaching, one of my central objectives was to reverse this balkanizing tendency. In my view, no subject is ever finished. No concept is sealed off from other concepts. Knowledge is continuous; ideas flow.

An example of this is something we at the Khan Academy call the knowledge map. By 2006, when I was tutoring my cousins and a handful of family friends, I had made about sixty question generators for various concepts, and I was beginning to have a hard time keeping track of my tutees' individual progress through the series. I had already been drawing graphlike structures on paper to illustrate which concepts were prerequisites for others, so I decided to write some software that would thread these together and automatically assign new exercises. It looked kind of cool once I had done my first pass, and I thought that my cousins might enjoy seeing the "map" of all the concepts in the system. It was a big hit with them and became a core piece of the Khan Academy software platform. In stressing the connections among subjects and giving learners a visual picture of where they've been and where they're going, we hope to encourage students to follow their own paths—to move actively up, down, and sideways, wherever their imaginations lead.

This—admittedly by a rather circuitous path—brings us back to the issue of personal responsibility.

Given that learning involves physical changes in each of our individual brains, and given that knowledge consists not of some linear progression but rather the gradually deepening comprehension of a vast web of concepts and ideas, a surprising corollary presents itself: No two educations are the same.

There is a very refreshing irony here. You can standardize curricula, but you can't standardize learning. No two brains are the same; no two pathways through the infinitely subtle web of knowledge are the same. Even the most rigorous standardized tests demonstrate only an approximate grasp of a certain subset of ideas that *each student understands in his or her own way.* Personal responsibility for learning goes hand in hand with a recognition of the uniqueness of each learner.

Filling in the Gaps

Do you wish to be great? Then begin by being. Do you desire to construct a vast and lofty fabric? Think first about the foundations of humility. The higher your structure is to be, the deeper must be its foundation.

—Saint Augustine

There is no such thing as a "perfect" learner.

There is no such thing as a student who "gets" every subject the first time through. In fact, most of the very brightest people I know enjoy revisiting basic ideas and seeing even deeper layers, fully realizing that they might never fully "get" most things. Even if there were someone with the potential to "get" everything, she would have to have had the extraordinary good luck to have nothing but excellent resources and teachers, to have gotten through her school years without being home with the flu, and to be improbably level in her focus and her moods. In the real world, this just doesn't happen. Every student, no matter how bright or how motivated, struggles now and then. Every student—even my cousin Nadia—is occasionally confused.

Every student forgets things or, by a combination of faulty teaching methods and human limitations, fails to grasp some crucial concepts and connections.

This less-than-tidy reality raises a number of questions. Can the inevitable gaps and lapses be repaired; and if so, how? Who bears the responsibility for recognizing the misconceptions and the stumbling places, and for putting in the time and effort to fix them?

I firmly believe that gaps in learning *can* be repaired, and moreover that they *must* be repaired if future, more advanced concepts are to be mastered. Subjects evolve one from another; one subject's climax is the starting point for the next. A gap or misconception in a previous subject therefore becomes a stumbling block in the one that follows.

But there's good news in this as well. We've noted that our brains seem to work most efficiently when aided by associations, by links. When a link is missing—say, for example, if we don't quite understand how simple division evolves into long division—we ourselves can often identify the source of the difficulty.

This suggests the seemingly obvious *how* of fixing gaps and lapses: Go back and revisit until the concept makes more sense; better still, try to actively apply the concept in a new context. Since neuroscience confirms our intuitive understanding that things are more easily learned the second time through, the review should not be onerous. Further, since repetition is an essential part of learning—a *physical* part of learning, in the creation and strengthening of neural pathways—this revisiting of a subject should result in a deeper and more durable grasp of it.

That part is simple. The harder question is this: Who is going to take the initiative and responsibility for seeing gaps and conducting reviews of past material to correct them?

In a standard classroom setting, it's very unlikely that the teacher will be able to identify every learning gap of each individual student. And even if he could, he would not be able to lead customized reviews on a case-by-case basis. There simply isn't enough classroom time for that, especially if the bulk of it is devoted to lecturing. Besides, the next unit is already looming. The class must move on.

By default, then, the ultimate responsibility for reviewing past lessons falls to the student. But will she follow through on this responsibility? Traditional classroom models make this difficult. The whole thrust of her education has taught her to be passive—to sit still, absorb, and eventually parrot back. Now she's being asked to be thoroughly proactive, to diagnose her own difficulties and actively see to their resolution. That's asking an awful lot of a student who has been trained to do the opposite.

Even if she can muster the clarity and the will to undertake an independent review of a troublesome subject, will she have access to the materials she needs? What if that material was in last year's textbook, now given back or discarded? What if she has some idea of what to look for but can't remember where to look? Clearly, there are difficulties here, and the difficulties work against the goal of helping students claim ownership of their own educations.

In principle, there is a fairly simple fix for this. The fix consists of two related strands.

First, students should be encouraged, at every stage of the learning process, to adopt an *active* stance toward their education. They shouldn't just take things in; they should figure things out. This is an extremely valuable habit to inculcate, since in the modern world of work no one tells you what formula to plug in; success lies in the ability to solve problems in novel and creative ways. Besides, if you think about it, asking kids to be active is nothing more than asking them to be their natural selves. Is it natural for kids to sit quietly for an hour, listening? No, it's natural for kids to want to *do* something, to be busy with work or play, to interact. Students are not naturally passive. Perversely, they need to be *taught* to be passive; the passivity then becomes a habit that makes them more tractable, perhaps, but less alert, less engaged in what they're doing. This trade-off may be helpful for maintaining order in a jam-packed conventional classroom, but that doesn't mean it's the best way for students to learn.

Active learning, *owned* learning, also begins with giving each student the freedom to determine where and when the learning will occur. This is the beauty of the Internet and the personal computer. If someone wants to study the quadratic equation on his back porch at 3 a.m., he can. If someone thinks best in a coffee shop or on the sideline of a soccer field, no problem. Haven't we all come across kids who seem bright and alert *except when they're in class*? Isn't it clear that there are morning people and night people? The radical portability of Internet-based education allows students to learn in accordance with their own personal rhythms, and therefore most efficiently.

Corollary to this is the idea of self-paced learning, which

gives the individual student control over *tempo*, as well as over where and when. The same person will learn at different rates on different days or when dealing with different subjects. But in a conventional classroom there is a single tempo tapped out by a single person—the teacher. Bound to this lockstep beat, the students who catch on quickest will soon become bored and zone out; perversely, they may even become discipline problems just as a way of keeping occupied. The students who need the most time will still be left behind. The tempo will be perfectly suited only for some hypothetical student in the middle of the curve. It's a case of one-size-fits-few.

With self-paced learning, by contrast, the tempo is right for every student because it is set by every student. If a given concept is easily grasped, one can sprint ahead, outrunning boredom. If a subject is proving difficult, it's possible to hit the pause button, or to go back and do more problems as necessary, without embarrassment and without asking the whole class to slow down.

Portability and self-pacing, then, are essential aids to active, self-motivated learning. For a student to truly take owner-ship of his education, however, there's another resource that's required: easy and ongoing access to the lessons that have come before. This is where Internet-based learning offers a huge advantage over textbooks and other conventional mate-rials. The lessons never disappear. Figuratively speaking, the blackboard is never erased, the books are never thrown away or given back. Students are encouraged to review because they can be confident that they will find what they are looking for, right there in their own computers. Even better, if the software knows when the student last visited a topic, it can directly make a review happen. This is analogous to your eleventh-grade biology teacher walking up to you in the hallway when you're in twelfth grade and asking you to explain photosynthesis.

Moreover, Internet-based learning has advantages not only for reviewing particular lessons, but for forging a deeper and more durable understanding of the associations *between* lessons. On the Internet we are not constrained by classroom walls, bells that dictate when a class is over, or state-mandated curricula. A topic can be covered in multiple ways though many different lenses across many superficially different subject areas.

This kind of learning fosters not only a deeper level of knowledge, but excitement and a sense of wonder as well. Nurturing this sense of wonder should be education's highest goal; failing to nurture it is the central tragedy of our current system.

PART 2

The Broken Model

Questioning Customs

Ignorance and a narrow education lay the foundation of vice, and imitation and custom rear it up.

—Mary Astell

The despotism of custom is everywhere the standing hindrance to human advancement.

—John Stuart Mill

Normal is what you're used to.

It seems to be a part of human nature that customs and institutions come to seem somehow inevitable and preordained. This sense, even when it is illusory, gives a stubborn staying power to habits and systems that have been around a while—even after it's become clear that they're no longer working very well. This is certainly the case with the educational system that most of us have known. It's so big that it's hard to see around it. It's so complexly integrated with other aspects of our culture that it's daunting to imagine a world without it.

If we are to muster the vision and the will to meaningfully

change education—to bring teaching and learning into closer alignment with the contemporary world as it really is—one of the leaps we need to make is to understand that the currently dominant educational model was not, in fact, inevitable. It is a human construct. It evolved along a certain pathway; other pathways were also possible. Parts of the system we now hold sacred—for example, the length of the class period or the number of years assigned to "elementary" or "high" school—are in fact rather arbitrary, even accidental. Things that are now considered orthodox were at various points regarded as controversial and radical.

Still, changing a system of such vast inertia and long tenure is clearly not easy. It's not just that tradition tends to cramp imagination; it's also that our educational system is intertwined with many other customs and institutions. Changing education would therefore lead to changes in other aspects of our society as well. It is my firm belief that over time this would be a very good thing; in the near term, however, such a prospect necessarily suggests disruptions and anxieties.

Let me offer an analogy that I hope will drive home the enormity of the challenge that we face. Consider something as basic as the habit of eating three meals a day.

Is there some biological imperative dictating that we should eat breakfast, lunch, and dinner versus two or four or five meals? Some Buddhist monks eat one meal a day at midday. There is some recent evidence that suggests alternate-day fasting might also be a healthy option.[1]

Why, then, do most of us cling to the habit of breakfast, lunch, and dinner, even though most of us today do much less manual labor than our ancestors who started this custom? The answer is simply this: It's what we've always done, just as we've always sent our kids to certain kinds of schools that operate in certain kinds of ways. It's a cultural habit that we take for granted.

Moreover, since we are social creatures and since our interwoven lives consist of many interconnected facets, the custom of three meals a day has become part of a matrix of many other activities. The workday allows for a lunch hour. Local economies depend on restaurants serving dinner, employing staff, collecting sales tax, and so forth. Insofar as families still sit down together, it is consensual mealtimes that most often bring them together.

For all these reasons, it would be exceedingly difficult to change the culture of breakfast, lunch, and dinner. The implications of such a change would be seismic. The whole rhythm of the workplace world would be altered. Entire industries would be challenged to adjust. Even the television schedule would need to shift.

As with our eating habits, so with our teaching habits.

Entire industries and some of our very largest professions depend on the persistence of our current system. Other social institutions—like giant publishers and test-prep companies— are synched to its workings. A certain teaching method implies certain goals and certain tests. The tests, in turn, have a serious impact on hiring practices and career advancement. Human nature being what it is, those who prosper under a given system tend to become supporters of that system. Thus the powerful tend to have a bias toward the status quo; our educational customs tend to perpetuate themselves, and because they inter-connect with so many other aspects of our culture, they are extraordinarily difficult to change.

Difficult, but not impossible. What's needed, in my view, is a perspective that allows us a fresh look at our most basic assumptions about teaching and learning, a perspective that takes nothing for granted and focuses on the simple but crucial questions of what works, what doesn't work, and why. To gain that perspective, it's helpful to look at the basics of our standard Western classroom model, to blow the dust off and to remind ourselves how the system came to be the way it is. It's also useful—and humbling—to realize that the debates and controversies currently surrounding education tend not to be new arguments at all; similar conflicts have been raging among people of passion and goodwill since teaching and learning began.

The basics of the standard educational model are remarkably stubborn and uniform: Go to a school building at seven or eight in the morning; sit through a succession of class periods of forty to sixty minutes, in which the teachers mainly talk and the students mainly listen; build in some time for lunch and physical exercise; go home to do homework. In the standard curriculum, vast and beautiful areas of human thought are artificially chopped into manageable chunks called "subjects." Concepts that should flow into one another like ocean currents are dammed up into "units." Students are "tracked" in a manner that creepily recalls Aldous Huxley's *Brave New World* and completely ignores the wonderful variety and nuance that distinguish human intelligence, imagination, and talent.

Such is the basic model—schematically simple in ways that mask or even deny the endless complexities of teaching and learning. For all its flaws, however, the standard model has one huge advantage over all other possible education methods: *It's there*. It's in place. It has tenure. The tendency is to believe that it *has* to be there.

Yet even the briefest survey of the history of education reveals that there is nothing inevitable or preordained about our currently dominant classroom model. Like every other system put in place by human beings, education is an invention, a work in progress. It has reflected, at various periods, the political, economic, and technological realities of its times, as well as the braking power of vested interests. In short, education has evolved, though not always in a timely manner, or before some unfortunate cohort of young people—a decade's worth? a generation's worth?—has been subjected to obsolete teachings that failed to prepare them for productive and successful futures.

It is time—past time—for education to evolve again. But if we hope to gain a clearer idea of where we need to go, it's useful to have at least a rudimentary awareness of where we've been.

Let's begin at the beginning. How did teaching start?

As it was succinctly put in a recent article by an educator named Erin Murphy in the Wharton School's online journal, the *Beacon*, the earliest forms of teaching and learning were essentially a case of "monkey see, monkey do." In preliterate hunter-gatherer societies, parents taught their children the basic survival skills by practicing them themselves and, whenever possible, inserting an element of play into the process. This form of teaching was simply an extension of the way other animals also taught their young. Lion cubs, for example, learn to hunt by mimicking the stalking postures and strategies of their parents, and turning the exercise into a game. In the case of both lions and early humans, the stakes in education were of the highest order. The offspring who learned their lessons well went on to prosper and reproduce. In the unforgiving environment of the savanna, the kids who didn't pay attention or never quite caught on were not around very long. To flunk was to perish.

As human language developed—language itself being a technology that radically changed and expanded our ways of sharing information—societies grew more complex and more specialized, and there came to be areas of desirable skills and knowledge that were beyond the abilities of parents alone to teach. This gave rise, at various times and in various forms, to the apprentice system. Significantly, the apprentice system marked the first time in human history that the main responsibility for education was shifted away from the family; this, of course, gave rise to a debate that has never yet died down about the respective roles of parents versus outside authorities in the education of children. Absent the bonds of family affection, the apprentice system was also the first time there was a clear, hierarchical distinction between the master/teacher and the apprentice/student. The master taught and ruled; the student submitted and learned.

Still, the manner of learning was a long way from the passive absorption of the more recent classroom model. Apprenticeship was based on *active* learning—learning by doing. The apprentice observed and mimicked the techniques and strategies of the master; in this regard, the apprentice system was a logical extension of learning by imitating a parent.

The apprentice system was also the world's first version of vocational school. It was a place to learn a trade—though in certain instances the trade in question could be extremely highbrow. Many associate the apprentice system with artisans like blacksmiths or carpenters, but it has also historically been the primary mode of education for future scholars and artists. In fact, even today's doctoral programs are really apprenticeships where a junior researcher (the PhD candidate) learns by doing research under and alongside a professor. Medical residency programs are also really apprenticeships.

Be that as it may, the apprentice system in general represented one side of a schism—those who believe that education should, above all, be practical, aimed at giving students the skills and information they need to make a living—that has existed for thousands of years, and exists still. On the other side are those who feel that seeking knowledge is an ennobling process worth pursuing for its own sake.

The preeminent representatives of this latter point of view were of course the Athenian Greeks of classical times. Plato, in the dialogue *Gorgias*, ascribes to Socrates, his alter ego and ideal man, the following statement: "Renouncing the honors at which the world aims, I desire only to know the truth." Clearly, there's a feisty and even defiant value judgment being made here, a slap at mere practicality. Aristotle, in the very first line of his *Metaphysics*, asserts that "all men naturally desire knowledge." He doesn't say marketable skills. He doesn't say the right credentials to get a job. He's talking about learning for the sake of learning, and he's positing that impulse as the very definition of what it means to be human. This is a long way from the model of apprenticeship as a way of learning to tan hides or carve stones or even treat patients.

There is much that is appealing in Plato's and Aristotle's pure approach to learning as a deep search for truth; this is, in fact, the mind-set that I hope to bring to students through my videos. However, there are a couple of serious problems with the model of the classic Greek academy. The first is that it was elitist—far more so than even today's most exclusive prep schools. The young men who could afford to hang around discussing the good and the true were oligarchs. Their families owned slaves. None of these students really needed to care about how to harvest crops or weave textiles. Real work, even work that was intellectual, was beneath them.

This led to a second, more destructive problem that still exists today. Once the pure search for truth was posited as the highest good, it followed that anything merely *useful* would be regarded as *less* good. Practical learning—learning that might actually help one do a job—was regarded as somehow dirty. And this prejudice pertained even to practical subjects—as, for example, finance or statistics—that are intellectually very rich and challenging.

As a classical legacy, this perceived separation between the truly intellectual and the merely useful was perpetuated by the

European universities during the Renaissance, then passed along to the early American colleges. The same set of biases persisted more or less intact well into the nineteenth century. Throughout this period, universities were generally something of an intellectual retreat for those who did not need to work in the traditional sense—future clergy, sons of the wealthy, and those devoting their lives to arts and letters (often enabled by the patronage of a wealthy family). Careers in even very intellectual professions, like law and medicine, were primarily developed *outside* the universities, through apprenticeships (although a few degree programs did begin to emerge in the eighteenth and nineteenth centuries). A law degree didn't become a mainstream credential in the United States until the late 1800s, when the completion of postgraduate instruction became a requirement for admission to the bar.[2] The idea that a college degree is a prerequisite to any professional career is a quite new one, only about a hundred years old. The idea that college is needed for *everyone* in order to be productive members of society is only a few decades old.

Let me be clear as to why I raise this point. I'm not suggesting that people shouldn't go to college. My contention, rather, is that universities and their career-seeking students have a deep-seated contradiction to resolve: On the one hand, our society now views a college education as a gateway to employment; on the other hand, academia has tended to maintain a bias against the vocational.

Clearly, our universities are still wrestling with an ancient but false dichotomy between the abstract and the practical, between wisdom and skill. Why should it prove so difficult to design a school that would teach both skill *and* wisdom, or even better, wisdom *through* skill? That's the challenge and the opportunity we face today.

But let's get back to some history.

In terms of making knowledge available to the many, the most important technology since spoken language has been written text. It has allowed for knowledge to exist and be collected outside a human mind. This allowed for information to persist unchanged over generations and for large amounts of information to be standardized and distributed (without the distributor having to memorize it).

Writing was a huge step forward, but it did come with unintended consequences. Whenever there is a hugely empowering new technology it can increase inequity between the haves that have access to it and the have-nots that don't. Early writings— whether it was on papyrus scrolls in ancient Egypt or in parchment books of the early Catholic Church—were nice for those who had access to them and knew how to read, but most people didn't. So the availability of written sources, far from eliminating the elitism and class distinctions that had gone before, actually exacerbated them for a time. The privileged now had greater supplies of special knowledge and therefore greater power.

And to make it clear how privileged a thing books were in their early days, think about how they had to be produced. They would be hand-copied by very specialized people with good penmanship. Consider how much it would cost to have one of the most educated people in your town spend a few years copying, say, the Bible, and you'll have a good sense of how expensive early books were—something on the order of a decent house in today's terms. So you can imagine that few people had access to touch them, much less the ability to read them.

Then came primitive block printing. Now a skilled artisan could carve text and images on the surface of a wooden block, dip it in ink, and press it onto a piece of paper. This was an advancement, but books were still expensive. Depending on the number of prints, this could actually be more labor-intensive than hand-copying text. It is hard to inflation-adjust the price of something over seven or eight centuries, but roughly based on the amount of labor involved, single books would have been comparable in cost to a nice luxury car—so well-off families might have a few, but they were by no means commonplace.

Then something epic happened in 1450 in Strasbourg, a German-speaking town that is now part of France. A fifty-two-year-old blacksmith named Johannes Gutenberg decided that he could simplify the creation of the blocks for printing text. Instead of each block being separately hand-carved, he realized that the individual letter blocks or "type" could be made in metal once and put together on a block for a given page. They could then be rearranged for the next page. Instead of multiple weeks of a skilled artisan's time being required to make a block for one page, it could now be done by a typesetter moving around type in a matter of a few hours—reducing labor costs by a factor of from ten to one hundred. Also, because the type was reused, more effort could be put into making the letters precise and uniform (thus the emergence of fonts). Because they were metal, instead of wood, they were more durable and the printing presses could be run faster. Now great works of writing would be accessible to many, many more people (although the first and only major work that Gutenberg printed at scale—the Gutenberg Bible—was still quite expensive for the time). Even more, it now became practical to print and distribute writings that weren't holy books or great works of classical literature—it is no coincidence that the first modern newspaper emerged in Gutenberg's Strasbourg roughly 150 years after the printing press.

In the spirit of not being Eurocentric, credit for the first movable type has to be given to the Chinese, who invented it a few hundred years before Gutenberg. He, however, was the first to create his type pieces out of materials similar to those used today. It also appears that movable type was able to spark more of a revolution in fifteenth-century Europe than in eleventh-century China and thirteenth-century Korea.

By the eighteenth century, movable type and the printing press had been perfected to the point that books were reasonably affordable. By the nineteenth century, what we now call textbooks had become viewed as a mainstay of mainstream education.

Pedagogically as well as politically, the broad distribution of textbooks raised new questions and difficulties—questions and difficulties that remain at the forefront of educational arguments today.

Before books were widely distributed, teaching was incredibly nonuniform. Teachers taught what they knew, in the manner that seemed best to them. Each teacher was therefore different, and when a teacher acquired a reputation for wisdom or originality or thrilling oratory—not necessarily accurate information—pupils flocked to him. Like a beloved village rabbi or priest, he was deemed to have something that could be gotten nowhere else. His students, in turn, came away with an education—and sometimes misinformation—unique to that particular classroom.

The mass production of books changed all that—and this is an aspect of education history to which too little attention has been paid. No longer was the teacher the sole source of information and the ultimate authority on a subject. Now there was an expert *behind* the expert, sharing in the teacher's prestige as the source of knowledge. The teacher ruled in the classroom but the textbook had standing in the world beyond. What if the teacher and the text disagreed? The legitimizing power of print seemed to give the last word to the book. On the other hand, textbooks empowered teachers to expose their students to the latest thinking from the broader world. They gave students the ability to study at their own pace and come to class ready to be engaged at a deeper level by a master teacher.

What is clear, however, is that it was the wide availability of books that ushered in the age of educational standardization. Suddenly students in distant places were reading the same poems and proverbs, learning the same historic dates and names of kings and generals, working out the same problems in arithmetic.

And standardization itself was not a bad thing. In a world growing more complex and gradually interconnected, standardization was a means to inclusion; it promised a leveling of the playing field and at least the potential for a true meritoc-racy. It also mitigated the impact of bad instruction that would otherwise go unchecked. Now students were less likely to be misled by a one-off viewpoint or inaccurate explanation.

The challenge, however—the same challenge in the early days of textbooks as now in the wider world of Internet-based learning—was this: How can we most effectively deploy stan-dardized learning tools without undermining the unique gifts of teachers?

The Prussian Model

*All greatness of character is dependent on individuality.
The man who has no other existence than that which
he partakes in common with all around him, will never
have any other than an existence of mediocrity.*

—JAMES FENIMORE COOPER

As we've seen, education through the ages took place in many different venues and by many different methods. Apprentices learned by doing in their masters' workshops. Classical Greeks walked around or sat under olive trees, exchanging viewpoints until the wine ran out. Early universities pursued esoteric topics for a handful of privileged people who'd done their early learning at home; most of those students were wealthy or connected enough that "work" was almost a dirty word.

That gives us a little context for higher education. But when and where did there come to be such a thing as "primary school" and "secondary school" as we know it (or K-12 education, as it is often now referred to)? The orthodoxies that we take for granted and are now in thrall to—the length of the school day and the school year; the division of the day into periods; the slicing of disciplines into "subjects"—where did these things come from? For that matter, who decided that education should be tax-supported and compulsory, that it should begin at a certain age and end after a certain number of "grades," and that it should be the business of the state to decide what should be taught and who could be a teacher?

To those not in the field, it may come as a surprise to learn that all these then-radical innovations in what we now call K-12 education were first put in place in eighteenth-century Prussia. Prussia—with its stiff whiskers, stiff hats, and stiff way of marching in lockstep—is where our basic classroom model was invented. Compulsory, tax-supported public education was seen as a political at least as much as a pedagogical tool, and no apology was made for this. The idea was not to produce independent thinkers, but to churn out loyal and tractable citizens who would learn the value of submitting to the authority of parents, teachers, church, and, ultimately, king. The Prussian philosopher and political theorist Johann Gottlieb Fichte, a key figure in the development of the system, was perfectly explicit about its aims. "If you want to influence a person," he wrote, "you must do more than merely talk to him; you must fashion him, and fashion him in such a way that he simply cannot will otherwise than what you wish him to will."

The standard classroom model offered boundless opportunities for political indoctrination. Some of these were direct and obvious, such as the manner in which subjects like history and social studies were presented. But there were also other, more subtle ways of shaping young minds. Former New York

State Teacher of the Year John Taylor Gatto has written that "the whole system was built on the premise that isolation from first-hand information and fragmentation of the abstract information presented by teachers would result in obedient and subordinate graduates." It was not by accident that whole ideas were broken up into fragmented "subjects." Subjects could be learned by rote memorization, whereas mastering larger ideas called for free and unbridled thinking.

Similarly, according to Gatto, our sacred notion of the "class period" was put in place "so that self-motivation to learn would be muted by ceaseless interruptions." Heaven forbid that students might delve beyond the prescribed curriculum or have time to discuss possibly heterodox and dangerous ideas among themselves; the bell rang and they had no choice but to break off their conversation or their deeper inquiry and move on to the next episode of approved instruction. By design, order trumped curiosity; regimentation took precedence over personal initiative.

Now, I don't personally believe that the Prussian system was designed purely as a tool for subjugation to the will of a ruling class. There were many aspects of it that were innovative and egalitarian for the time. In fact, just the notion of a universal, tax-funded, mandatory public education system was revolutionary. It lifted millions into the middle class and played no small part in Germany's rise as an industrial power. And the most economical way to deliver education to *everyone*, given the technology at the time, may have been the Prussian model. However, whether it was intentional or not, the system tended to stifle deeper inquiry and independent thought. In the 1800s, high-level creative and logical thinking may not have been as important as a disciplined tractability coupled with basic skills, but two hundred years later, they clearly are.

In the first half of the nineteenth century, the Prussian system was put in place in the United States with few modifications, largely due to the influence of Horace Mann, then the Secretary of Education for the state of Massachusetts. His motivations were generally forward-thinking for the time; he wanted to provide a solid basic education to students of all socioeconomic ranks. As in Prussia, this would play a significant role in building a middle class capable of filling the jobs of a booming industrial sector. There was, however, also an element of indoctrination that had positives and negatives depending on your point of view. While it would be beyond the scope of this book to examine in detail the political climate of the time, suffice it to say that in the 1840s—as today—the United States was faced with the issue of "Americanizing" large groups of immigrants from many disparate cultures.

By 1870, all thirty-seven states had public schools and the United States had become one of the most literate countries in the world.[3] Although the most fundamental ideas of the Prussian model—students separated by age moving in lockstep, bells ringing—had become commonplace, there was not yet a lot of standardization across the country as to what the students were taught and for how many years they needed to be educated.

To address this issue, the National Education Association formed the "Committee of Ten" in 1892. This was a group of educators—primarily university presidents—led by Charles Eliot, the president of Harvard, whose mission was to determine what primary and secondary education should be like. It was these ten men who decided that everyone in the United States should—starting at age six and ending at age eighteen—have eight years of elementary education followed by four years of high school. They decided that English, math, and reading should be covered every year, while chemistry and physics should be introduced near the end of high school.

For the most part, the recommendations of the Committee of Ten were refreshingly progressive for the time. For example, the committee felt that every student should get a fair chance to see if he had an interest in and capacity for intellectual work. In most of the world—and this is still true today—subjects like trigonometry, physics, or literature were reserved for the very top students destined for professional careers; the bulk of students were tracked into purely vocational courses around eighth grade. I also really like what they had to say about teaching math, the spirit of which has been lost in many of today's schools. For example, regarding geometry:

As soon as the student has acquired the art of rigorous demonstration, his work should cease to be merely receptive. He should begin to devise constructions and demonstrations for himself. Geometry cannot be mastered by reading the demonstrations of a text-book, and while there is no branch of elementary mathematics in which purely receptive work, if continued too long, may lose its interest more completely, there is also none in which independent work can be made more attractive and stimulating.

In other words, if you want students to really learn geometry, you can't just have them listen, read, and repeat. You have to allow students to explore the subject on their own.

For all their comparative enlightenment, however, the Committee of Ten lived in a world without interstate highways, the Federal Reserve, television, awareness of DNA, or air travel except in balloons, not to mention computers and the Internet. The system they framed has not been fundamentally rethought in 120 years, and it has by now taken on such a weight of orthodoxy and rust as to stifle the sincere creative efforts of even the best-meaning teachers and administrators.

The heavy baggage of the current academic model has become increasingly apparent recently, as economic realities no longer favor a docile and disciplined working class with just the basic proficiencies in reading, math, and the liberal arts. Today's world needs a workforce of creative, curious, and self-directed lifelong learners who are capable of conceiving and implementing novel ideas. Unfortunately, this is the type of student that the Prussian model actively suppresses.

Arguments about education are contentious enough without bringing partisan politics into them, but it is interesting to note in passing that in recent years our Prussian-based public school model has come under virulent attack from both the right and the left. Conservative complaints tend to center on the alleged usurpation by government of choices and prerogatives more properly left to parents; as it was put by author Sheldon Richman in his book *Separating School and State: How to Liberate American Families*, "the state's apparently benevolent goal of universal education has actually been an insidious effort to capture all children in its net."

Attacks from the left have tended to be surprisingly similar in tone, though the villain is not the government but the corporations that have the most to gain from a well-behaved and conformist population. Writing in the September 2003 issue of *Harper's*, John Taylor Gatto urged that we "wake up to what our schools really are: laboratories of experimentation on young minds, drill centers for the habits and attitudes that corporate society demands.... School trains children to be employees and consumers."[4]

The foregoing is not intended as a wholesale condemnation of our current educational system. I'm not proposing that we shut down the schools and start over. What I am suggesting, however, is that we adopt a more questioning and skeptical stance toward the educational customs and assumptions we've inherited. Those customs, as I hope I've made clear, were the products of particular times and circumstances, established by human beings with human flaws and limited wisdom, whose motives were often complicated. That doesn't mean there aren't some good ideas in our traditional approach. Most people who've been to school, after all, can read and write, know some basic math and science, and hopefully have picked up some useful social skills as well. To that extent, school works. But we do ourselves and our kids a disservice if we fail to look past those minimum requirements and recognize the places where the system has become creaky and archaic, and why old customs and standards no longer suffice.

Swiss Cheese Learning

As we've seen, our current system divides disciplines into "subjects," and further divides the subjects into independent units, thereby creating the dangerous illusion that the topics are discrete and unconnected. While that's a serious problem, there's an even more basic failing here: Chances are that the topics themselves have not been covered thoroughly enough, because our schools measure out their efforts in increments of time rather than in target levels of mastery. When the interval allotted for a given topic has run out, it's time to give a test and move on.

Let's consider a few things about that inevitable test. What constitutes a passing grade? In most classrooms in most schools, students pass with 75 or 80 percent. This is customary. But if you think about it even for a moment, it's unacceptable if not disastrous. Concepts build on one another. Algebra requires arithmetic. Trigonometry flows from geometry. Calculus and physics call for all of the above. A shaky understanding early on will lead to complete bewilderment later. And yet we blithely give out passing grades for test scores of 75 or 80. For many teachers, it may seem like a kindness or perhaps merely an administrative necessity to pass these marginal students. In effect, though, it is a disservice and a lie. We are telling students they've learned something that they really *haven't* learned. We wish them well and nudge them ahead to the next, more difficult unit, for which they have not been properly prepared. We are setting them up to fail.

Forgive a glass-half-empty sort of viewpoint, but a mark of 75 percent means you are missing fully one-quarter of what you need to know (and that is assuming it is on a rigorous assessment). Would you set out on a long journey in a car that had three tires? For that matter, would you try to build your dream house on 75 or 80 percent of a foundation?

It's easy to rail against passing students whose test scores are marginal. But I would press the argument further and say that even a test score of 95 should not be regarded as good enough, as it will inevitably lead to difficulties later on.

Consider: A test score of 95 almost always earns an A, but it also means that 5 percent of some important concept has not been grasped. So when the student moves on to the next concept in the chain, she's already working with a 5 percent deficit. Even worse, many deficiencies have been masked by tests that have been dumbed down to the point that students can get 100 percent without any real understanding of the underlying concept (they require only formula memorization and pattern matching).

Continuing our progression through another half dozen concepts—which might bring our hypothetical student to, say, Algebra II or Pre-Calc. She's been a "good" math student all along, but all of a sudden, no matter how much she studies and how good her teacher is, she has trouble comprehending what is happening in class.

How is this possible? She's gotten A's. She's been in the top quintile of her class. And yet her preparation lets her down. Why? The answer is that our student has been a victim of Swiss cheese learning. Though it seems solid from the outside, her education is full of holes.

She's been tested and tested, but the tests have lacked rigor and any deficiencies they identified weren't corrected. She's been given gold stars for her 95s—or even 100s—on superficial exams, and that's fine; there's nothing wrong with giving kids gold stars. But she should *also* have been given a review of the 5 percent of problems that she missed. The review should have been followed by a rigorous retest; if the retest resulted in anything less than 100 percent, the process should have been repeated. Once a certain level of proficiency is obtained, the learner should attempt to teach the subject to other students so that they themselves develop a deeper understanding. As they progress, they should keep revisiting the core ideas through the lenses of different, active experiences. That's the way to get the holes out of Swiss cheese learning. It is, after all, much better and more useful to have a deep understanding of algebra than a superficial understanding of algebra, trigonometry, and calculus. Students with deep backgrounds in algebra find calculus intuitive.

As a practical matter, our conventional classroom model does not generally allow for these customized reviews and retests, still less for moving beyond memorization to experience the concepts through open-ended, creative projects. This is one of the central ways in which the model proves archaic and no longer serves our needs.

The example of the historically good student all of a sudden not understanding an advanced class because of a Swiss cheese foundation could best be termed hitting a wall. And it is commonplace. We have all seen classmates go through this and have directly experienced it ourselves. It's a horrible feeling, leaving the student only frustration and helplessness.

Let's look at a couple of subjects where students—even previously very successful students—classically hit the wall. One of these is organic chemistry—a discipline that has converted generations of pre-med students into English majors. Is organic chemistry more difficult than freshman general chemistry? Yes—that's why it comes after. But at the same time it's just an extrapolation of the concepts in the first-year course. If you truly understand inorganic chemistry, then organic makes *intuitive* sense. But absent a firm grasp of the basics, organic chemistry doesn't feel intuitive at all; rather, it seems like a daunting, dizzying, and endless progression of reactions that need to be memorized. Faced with such a mind-numbing chore, many students give up. Some, by superhuman effort, power through. The problem is that memorization without intuitive understanding can't remove the wall, but only push it back.

An even more vivid example of the power of Swiss cheese learning to wreak havoc is provided by calculus—possibly the most common subject on which students meet their Waterloo. This is not because calculus is fundamentally so difficult. It is because calculus is a synthesis of much that has gone before. It assumes complete mastery of algebra and trigonometry. Calculus has the power to solve problems that are beyond the reach of more elementary forms of math, but unless you've truly understood those more elementary concepts, calculus is of no use to you. It's this element of synthesis, of pulling it all together, that gives calculus its beauty. At the same time, however, it's why calculus is so likely to reveal the cracks in people's math foundations. In stacking concept upon concept, calculus is the subject most likely to tip the balance, reveal the dry rot, and send the whole edifice crashing down.

Another consequence of Swiss cheese learning is the very common but perplexing inability of many people—even very bright people with top-tier educations—to connect what they have studied in the classroom to questions they encounter in the outside world. Examples of this abound in everyday life; let me present one such instance from my own experience as a hedge fund analyst.

My work in that capacity consisted partly in interviewing CEOs and CFOs of publicly traded companies so that I could understand their businesses well enough to make informed predictions about their future performance. One day I asked a CFO why his company's marginal cost of production seemed higher than that of its competitors. (The marginal cost of production refers to the expense of creating one extra unit of a product, before the "fixed costs" of a factory and other corporate overhead have been figured in. In other words, it's the labor and materials price of that one single widget.) The CFO looked at me—a tad suspiciously, as if he imagined that some sort of corporate espionage might be afoot—and told me that information about marginal cost was considered proprietary, and he had no idea where I'd come up with my number.

I told him that he'd given me that number himself.

He scratched his chin, crossed and uncrossed his ankles.

I pointed out that included in the company's publicly stated filings were numbers for the cost of goods sold from two different periods, along with reports of the number of units sold. Figuring out the marginal cost of production, then, was a matter of doing a little elementary math—specifically, solving two equations with two unknowns, a type of problem that is the stuff of eighth-grade algebra.

Now, I tell this story not to embarrass or criticize the CFO. He was a bright guy with an Ivy League education, and his math background extended to calculus and beyond. Clearly, though, there seemed to be something wrong, something missing, in the way that he'd been taught. He'd apparently studied algebra with an eye toward getting a good grade on the test that was the climax of the unit; presumably the test centered on the working out of a handful of problems, and the problems consisted of solving for variables that had no apparent meaning in the real world. What, then, was the *point* of learning algebra? What was algebra actually *about*? What could algebra *do*? These very basic questions, it seemed, had gone unexplored.

This failure to relate classroom topics to their eventual application in the real world is one of the central shortcomings of our broken classroom model, and is a direct consequence of our habit of rushing through conceptual modules and pronouncing them finished when in fact only a very shallow level of functional understanding has been reached. What do most kids actually take away from algebra? Sadly, the usual takeaway is that it's about a bunch of x's and y's, and that if you plug in a few formulas and procedures that you've learned by rote, you'll come up with the answer.

But the power and importance of algebra is not to be found in x's and y's on a test paper. The important and wonderful thing is that all those x's and y's can stand in for an infinitely diverse set of phenomena and ideas. The same equations that I used to figure out the production costs of a public company could be used to calculate the momentum of a particle in space. The same equations can model both the optimal path of a projectile and the optimal price for a new product. The same ideas that govern the chances of inheriting a disease also inform whether it makes sense to go for a first down on fourth-and-inches.

The difficulty, of course, is that getting to this deeper, functional understanding would use up valuable class time that might otherwise be devoted to preparing for a test. So most students, rather than appreciating algebra as a keen and versatile tool for navigating through the world, see it as one more hurdle to be passed, a *class* rather than a gateway. They learn it, sort of, then push it aside to make room for the lesson to follow.

Tests and Testing

Let's now look at another aspect and some other implications of our long and largely unexamined habits of classroom teaching and testing. To do this, let's start by asking one of those incredibly basic questions: What do tests really test?

At first glance this question might seem so simple as to be trivial, but the longer and deeper you look at it, the less self-evident the answer becomes.

Consider some things that tests *don't* test.

Tests say little or nothing about a student's *potential* to learn a subject. At best, they offer a snapshot of where the student stands at a given moment in time. Since we have seen that students learn at widely varying rates, and that catching on faster does not necessarily imply understanding more deeply, how meaningful are these isolated snapshots?

Tests say nothing about how long learning will be retained. Recalling what we've learned about how the brain stores information, retention involves the effective transfer of knowledge from short-term memory to long-term memory. Some students seem to have a knack for keeping facts and figures and formulas in short-term memory just exactly as long as they need them for a grade. After that, who knows? Conventional testing doesn't tell us.

Testing tells us little or nothing about the *why* of right or wrong answers. In a given instance, does a mistake suggest an important concept missed or only a moment's carelessness? If a student fails to finish an exam, did she give up in frustration or simply run out of time? Given the time she needed, how well might she have done? On the other hand, what does a correct answer tell us about a student's quality of reasoning? Was the correct answer the result of deep understanding, a brilliant intuition, rote memorization, or a lucky guess? Usually it's impossible to tell.

Finally, tests are by their nature partial and selective. Say a particular module has covered concepts A through G. The test—by design or by randomness—mainly addresses concepts B, D, and F. The students who, on a hunch or by sheer dumb luck, have geared their preparation toward that subset of the subject matter will probably test much better. Does this suggest greater mastery of the *entire* subject? Again, given traditional classroom approaches, there's just no way to know.

So then, coming back to our original question—what do tests actually test?—it seems that the most that can be confidently said is this: Tests measure the *approximate* state of a student's memory and *perhaps* understanding, in regard to a particular subset of subject matter at a given moment in time, it being understood that the measurement can vary considerably and randomly according to the particular questions being asked.

That's a pretty modest statement of what we should reasonably expect to glean from testing, but I would argue that it's all that the data justify. To be sure, the data could and should be improved; as we'll see, broadening and deepening the range of what we can learn from students' exercises and test results is at the very heart of the improvements I would propose to our current system. For now, however, suffice it to say that our over-reliance on testing is based largely on habit, wishful thinking, and leaps of faith.

For all of that, conventional schools tend to place great emphasis on test results as a measure of a student's innate ability or potential—not only on standardized tests, but on thoroughly *un*standardized end-of-term exams that may or may not be well designed—and this has very serious consequences. What are we actually accomplishing when we hand out those A's and B's and C's and D's? As we've seen, what we're *not* accomplishing is meaningfully measuring student potential. On the other hand, what we're doing very effectively is labeling kids, squeezing them into categories, defining and often limiting their futures.

This outcome is actually what the Prussian architects of our standard classroom model explicitly intended. Tests determined who would go to school beyond eighth grade and who would not. This, in turn, would dictate who was eligible for the more prestigious and remunerative professions, and who would be consigned to a lifetime of menial labor and low social status. Early industrial society needed a lot of lower-end workers, after all, people who worked with their hands and backs rather than their minds. The Prussian version of "tracking" students assured a plentiful labor supply. Moreover, since the testing process, for all its flaws and limitations, could claim to be "scientific" and objective, there was at least the illusion of fairness in the system. If you didn't look too closely—if you factored out things like family wealth and political connections and the wherewithal to hire private tutors—the system could pass for a meritocracy.

To be clear, I am not antitesting. Tests can be valuable diagnostic tools to identify gaps in learning that need to be fixed. Well-designed tests can also be used as evidence that someone actually knows a subject domain well at a specific point in time. What is important to remember, however, is to have a solid dose of skepticism when interpreting results from even the most well-designed tests; they are, after all, just imperfect human constructs.

Tests also change. If the changes could be solely ascribed to evolving insights into educational methods, that would be great. In the real world, however, things are seldom so straightforward. Economics and politics factor in, as does a strange Alice-in-Wonderland kind of cockeyed logic; tests change, in part, so that the results will come closer to what the testers think they should be.

In a fascinating recent instance of this, the state of New York hired a new company to redesign the standardized tests administered to millions of third through eighth graders.[5] Why the expensive overhaul? Two seemingly contradictory reasons. In 2009, the *old* tests seemed to have become too predictable, so that students and teachers, having a pretty good idea of what was coming, were doing mere test prep rather than real teaching and learning. Test scores were high…*too* high to be considered reliable. Responding to criticism regarding the perceived laxity of their standards, the New York State Board of Regents ordered its then–testing company to make the tests more difficult. It complied, and perhaps did too good a job; scores plummeted. To state what should be obvious, teachers didn't get less good and students didn't get less smart from one year to the next. So who was really being tested here—the students or the testers?

Apparently the testers flunked, because the state fired them and hired a different company, giving the new designers an extremely specific set of guidelines. Questions should not be "tricky." Possibly misleading use of negatives—"Which of the following words cannot be used to describe the tone of this passage?"—was disallowed, as were those old standbys "none of the above" or "all of the above." So finicky had the regents become that they even specified the fonts that should be used for maximum legibility. Moreover, they mandated that reading samples should "have characters that are portrayed as positive role models [and] have a positive message." What all this positivity has to do with any sort of objective measure of reading competence is too subtle for me. Clearly, this is politics, not pedagogy.

Were the new tests more reliable than the old tests? I have no idea. And that's really the point. It's awfully difficult to appraise the quality of tests *except by way of the test results*. Are they reasonably consistent? Do they more or less conform to what experts *think* they should be? What politicians *want* them to be? It's all rather circular. Again, I don't deny the importance of testing, and I'm certainly not suggesting we do away with it. What I'm urging, though, is a measure of skepticism and caution in how much weight we give to test results alone. The accuracy and meaningfulness of test results should never be taken for granted.

Tracking Creativity

In our own, more politically sensitive—or perhaps more hypocritical—time, people don't openly talk about curtailing the educational opportunities of a large part of the population so as to assure a large and docile supply of manual workers. Besides, manual workers are no longer what society needs; increasingly, all around the world, *mind* workers are what's called for. Still, our educational model, with its deeply flawed system of testing and grading, effectively deprives many students of the chance to reach their full potential. They are labeled early and treated accordingly.

Whether the process is called *tracking* or whether it's known by some kinder, gentler (and less honest) name, the upshot is the same. It's a process of *exclusion*, which is exactly the opposite of what our schools should be trying to accomplish. To be successful in a competitive and interconnected world, we need every mind we have; to solve our common problems regarding relations among peoples and the health of our planet, we need all the talent and imagination we can find. What sense does it make to effectively *filter out* a percentage of kids so early in the game, to send the message that they probably have nothing to contribute? What about the late bloomers? What about the possible geniuses who happen to look at problems differently from most of us and may not test well at an early age?

Let's stay for a moment with this notion of *differentness* when it comes to problem-solving. Isn't this simply another way of defining creativity? In my view, that's exactly what it is, and the troubling fact is that our current system of testing and grading tends to filter out the creative, *different-thinking* people who are most likely to make major contributions to a field.

An entire book could be written about education and creativity: how to measure it, how to foster it, and whether it can be taught at all. The bottom line is that we know it when we see it. It is that ability to see something in an entirely new way, to create something from scratch, to explore ideas that never existed before. It also transcends subject matter and variety of expertise. Bob Dylan is massively creative, but so was Isaac Newton. Pablo Picasso saw the world in ways that it had never been seen before, but so did Richard Feynman. Or Marie Curie. Or Steve Jobs.

There are two related points I'm driving at here. The first is that creativity in general tends to be egregiously under-appreciated and often selected against in our schools. The second point—and in my view this is nothing short of tragic—is that many educators fail to see math, science, and engineering as "creative" fields at all.

Even as our world is being daily transformed by breathtaking innovations in science and technology, many people continue to imagine that math and science are mostly a matter of memorizing formulas to get "the right answer." Even engineering, which is in fact the process of creating something from scratch or putting things together in novel and non-self-evident ways, is perplexingly viewed as a mechanical or rote subject. This viewpoint, frankly, could only be held by people who never truly learned math or science, who are stubbornly installed on one side of the so-called Two Culture divide. The truth is that anything significant that happens in math, science, or engineering is the result of heightened intuition and creativity. This is art by another name, and it's something that tests are not very good at identifying or measuring. The skills and knowledge that tests *can* measure are merely warm-up exercises.

Consider an analogy. Imagine if we assessed student dancers purely by their flexibility or their strength. If we judged student painters purely by their ability to mix colors perfectly or draw exactly what they see. If we appraised aspiring writers purely by their mastery of grammar or vocabulary. What would we actually be measuring? At best, we'd be measuring certain attributes and prerequisites that would be helpful or necessary for the practice of these respective crafts. Would the measurements say anything about an individual's potential for true artistry? For greatness? No.

The situation is similar in science and mathematics and engineering. It's true that one is unlikely to get very far in those fields without a good grasp of the basics—the grammar and vocabulary, if you will, of those disciplines. But it does not follow that the "best-performing" student—that is, the one with the greatest facility for catching on quickly *at a certain level of understanding*, and therefore the one with the highest test scores—will necessarily end up as the most accomplished scientist or engineer. That will depend on creativity, passion, and originality—things that begin where testing leaves off.

The danger of using assessments as reasons to filter out students, then, is that we may overlook or discourage those whose talents are of a different order—whose intelligence tends more to the oblique and the intuitive. At the very least, when we use testing to exclude, we run the risk of squelching creativity before it has a chance to develop.

Recall for a moment the case of my cousin Nadia and her botched math placement test. Nadia was lucky. Her parents were involved and proactive; her school was attentive and responsive. If things had worked out just a little less well, Nadia would have been excluded from her best chance to learn higher math. She would have been labeled one of the less smart kids, and a whole chain of negative consequences would have emerged from that. Her own confidence would have been shaken. Teachers' expectations of her would have been lowered and, human nature being what it is, her self-expectations would probably have followed. Chances are she would have gotten less effective teachers after that, since the brightest and most motivated teachers tend to work with the "fastest" classes, and the "slow" kids get...well, the slow classes.

And all of this might have happened because of one snapshot test, administered on one morning in the life of a twelve-year-old girl—a test that didn't even test what it purported to be testing! The exam, remember, claimed to be measuring math *potential*—that is, *future* performance. Nadia did poorly on it because of one *past* concept that she'd misunderstood. She has cruised through every math class she's ever taken since (she took calculus as a sophomore in high school). What does this say about the meaningfulness and reliability of the test? Yet we look to exams like this to make crucial, often irreversible, and deceptively "objective" decisions regarding the futures of our kids.

Homework

In our current muddled and contentious state of play when it comes to education, it seems that *anything* can become a battleground for competing ideologies and strongly held opinions, whether or not those opinions can be backed up by solid evidence or data. So I have found it fascinating to follow recent controversies regarding homework—a seemingly benign topic that has lately given rise to passionate if not necessarily well-informed arguments.

A recent article in the *New York Times* opened with a bit of domestic drama:

> After Donna Cushlanis's son kept bursting into tears midway through his second-grade math problems, which one night took over an hour, she told him not to do all of his homework.
>
> "How many times do you have to add seven plus two?" [the mother] asked. "I have no problem with doing homework, but that put us both over the edge."[6]

It so happened that Ms. Cushlanis was a secretary at the suburban school district of Galloway, New Jersey, and she spoke of her qualms about her second grader's homework burden to the superintendent of schools. The superintendent assured her that the district was already in the midst of reevaluating its homework policies, and was considering new guidelines limiting homework to ten minutes for each school grade; that is, ten minutes a night for first graders, twenty minutes for second graders, and so on. This approach, at the very least, seemed tidy and systematic...but what was it really based on? Why should teachers and administrators feel confident that this was the right amount of homework?

What *is* the right amount of homework? This seems like a simple enough question. It isn't. So let's let it simmer awhile while we pursue our discussion.

The homework battle that was going on in Galloway, New Jersey, seemed to summarize a controversy that was brewing everywhere. For every parent like Ms. Cushlanis, who believed her child was being unduly and unhealthily stressed, there was an equally caring parent who felt that her child's education was inadequate and lacking in rigor. "Most of our kids can't spell without spell check or add unless it comes up on the computer," said one such mom, quoted in the *Times* article. "If we coddle them when they're younger, what happens when they get into the real world?"

Some Galloway parents claimed that excessive homework constituted a sort of "second shift" of school, an unreasonable preemption of time that should be used for playing, socializing, finding pollywogs. Against this viewpoint, one adult voiced the somewhat dated but nevertheless sincere conviction that "part of growing up is having a lot of homework every day. You're supposed to say, 'I can't come out and play because I have to stay in and do homework.'"

As it was in suburban New Jersey, so it was in school districts around the country and the world. Some people argued for more homework, some for less. Various experimental programs were put in place. Some schools made homework "optional." Some schools put aggregate limits on homework, which created a nightmarish chore for teachers who had to coordinate how much they assigned. Some school districts essentially played semantic games, now calling after-school assignments "goal work" rather than homework. Other schools banned homework on weekends or before vacation breaks; some took the interesting step of forbidding homework on the evening before major standardized exams, perhaps sending the message that it was okay for kids to be stressed and exhausted except when taking tests that might reflect on the performance of the school itself.

Nor was all this angst and uncertainty about homework restricted to U.S. schools. At a time when test results are compared globally, and cross-border college and even prep school applications are at an all-time high, the anxiety and contention were contagious. In Toronto, an edict banned homework for kindergartners and for older kids on school holidays. The controversy reached as far as the Philippines, where the education department opposed weekend assignments so kids could enjoy their childhoods.

Interestingly, students themselves seemed to disagree as virulently as their parents and teachers about the proper amounts and uses of homework. The *New York Times* education blog, "The Learning Network," invited middle-schoolers and teens to weigh in on the subject.[7] The preponderance of the posts, not surprisingly, were complaints about having too much still to do when the school day was over. Yet even allowing for some adolescent overstatement and melodrama, a few of the comments were disturbing if not heartbreaking. One ninth-grade girl wrote that "I came home at 4 pm and finished homework by 2 am. We couldn't go to dinner because I had too much homework. I couldn't talk to my Mom, Dad, or sister....So yes. I think I have too much homework. And no. It doesn't really help....I just copied everything I saw without any of the actual information being absorbed just to be done with the work. Homework ruined my life."

Distressingly, a recurring motif in the student comments was the subject of sleep deprivation. One seventh grader reported that she was routinely doing homework "until at least midnight. It's just too much!...It's just not healthy to get 6–7 hours of sleep each night." (Children up to age twelve, according to the National Sleep Foundation, should have ten to eleven hours of sleep per night. Teenagers require around nine and a quarter.) Another middle-schooler complained that "the whole year, our LA [language arts] teacher has taught us how to get by on 6 hours of sleep [and to] drain our brains dry of creative [thinking]." It's a little difficult to imagine what pedagogical purpose is served by having a generation of kids sleepwalk through their preteen and early teenage years.

Not all the student respondents were clamoring for less homework. Some were asking for *better* homework—challenging, meaningful assignments rather than the "busywork" that was often handed out. If the initiative shown by these students was heartening, it also pointed out a little-discussed deficiency in our traditional way of training teachers. According to a journal article called "Teacher Assessment of Homework," by a researcher named Stephen Aloia, the rather surprising fact was that "most teachers do not take courses specifically on homework during teacher training."[8] Lesson plans, yes; techniques for guiding classroom activities, yes; homework, no. It's as if homework is an afterthought, some strange gray area that is still the responsibility of students but not so much for teachers. According to Harris Cooper, author of *The Battle over Homework*, when it comes to crafting homework assignments, "most teachers are winging it." No wonder homework is sometimes seen by students—and parents—as a tedious waste of time.

On the other hand, when homework is demanding and meaningful, some students, at least, appreciate the difference. One high school junior commented in the *Times* blog that "at my old school, I got a lot more homework. At my new prep school I get less. The difference: I spend much more time on my homework at my current school because it is harder. I feel as if I actually accomplish something with the harder homework."

This sentiment was echoed by the same seventh grader who complained about being up until midnight every night. "We should be getting harder work, not more work!"

Given the eminent reasonableness of this suggestion, why do so many of our schools continue to focus on the quantity of homework rather than the quality? In part, the reason is simply that quantity, by definition, is easy to measure; quality is a far more subtle concept. Send kids home with four hours of homework, and you have at least a simulacrum of academic rigor.

But the more interesting question is why we have adopted this pile-it-on mentality in the first place. There is a swinging pendulum when it comes to attitudes about homework, and that pendulum has been in more or less constant motion for at least a hundred years. At the dawn of the twentieth century, the main purpose of homework was thought to be "training the mind" for the largely clerical, repetitive kinds of jobs that the trend toward urbanization and office work required; thus the emphasis was on memory drills, pattern recognition, rules of grammar—things that disciplined the mind but did not necessarily expand it. In the Progressive Era of the 1920s there was a reaction against this; rote memorization went out of fashion in favor of creative problem solving and self-expression. During the 1940s, homework was briefly out of vogue altogether, and this was probably a consequence of wartime. Young men were being sent off to die; let them enjoy their childhoods in the meantime.

Then in the 1950s came an event that, in the United States at least, created a crisis of national self-esteem and a panic regarding our educational methods and standards. That event was the launching of Sputnik. The Soviets had put a satellite into space. They had succeeded where the United States failed. They had won a contest in which each nation had invested a great deal of capital, both financial and psychological.

In terms of practical consequences, the "space race" turned out to be little more than a propaganda opportunity for whichever side seemed to be winning at a given moment. In the wake of the Sputnik embarrassment, however, one thing seemed absolutely clear: American kids were falling behind and needed to do more science homework.

In retrospect, this response—and certainly its virulence— was a little screwy; at the same time, it provides a vivid and chastening example of how adults tend to project their anxieties onto their children. Had Soviet *kids* launched Sputnik? Had American *kids* made U.S. rockets crash on the launchpad? The space race in those years was largely a contest between the scientists that each side had inherited from Germany and Hungary in the wake of World War II; what did kids have to do with it? Then too, the Soviet Union was dedicating a far larger share of its GDP to rocketry and the military. No matter. As was widely reported and endlessly repeated, Soviet kids, from the age of nine onward, were doing twice as much math and science homework as their American peers.[9]

Clearly, America's national prestige if not the very survival of democracy depended on closing the homework gap. In the late 1950s and early 1960s, kids went home with a lot of crisp new biology and physics textbooks, and ground down a lot of Number 2 pencils working endless problems in introductory algebra, geometry, and especially trigonometry, which was useful for working out the trajectory of missiles.

Not surprisingly, the homework pendulum soon swung back. By the mid-1960s, homework was coming "to be seen as a symptom of excessive pressure on students.... Learning theories again questioned the value of homework and raised its possible detrimental consequences for mental health."[10]

True to the pattern, however, homework rose again during the next U.S. crisis of confidence—the spasm of worry occasioned by the economic rise of Japan in the early 1980s. As with Sputnik, Japan's success led to a flurry of sincere if sometimes misdirected national soul-searching. What were *they* doing right that *we* were doing wrong? Was it their consensual management style? Their relentless work ethic? Were they just plain smarter? Maybe it had to do with...homework!

Inconveniently, however, studies showed that Japanese students did not do more homework than their American counterparts; in fact they did less. This was puzzling, but it turned out to be only one of many seeming anomalies that kept cropping up in comparative international studies.

Among the nations whose students ranked near the top of international test results, some, like South Korea and Taiwan, did in fact assign a lot of homework. (This would also seem to be the case with China, though reliable statistics regarding that nation are hard to come by.) But other equally high-scoring countries—Denmark and Czechoslovakia (as it was then called), in addition to Japan—assigned very little. Then there were some very homework-heavy nations—Greece, Thailand, Iran—whose students tested poorly. France, whose students tested roughly as well as their U.S. counterparts, reportedly sent its middle-schoolers home with twice as much homework. And meanwhile, well before the turn of the new millennium, the all-time heavyweight champion of homework, the Soviet Union, had gone out of business altogether.

What is one to make of all this contradictory and chaotic data? Speaking as an engineer and recovering hedge fund analyst, I would argue that the only conclusion that can be logically drawn is this: The amount of homework assigned—if considered without reference to a raft of many other complicating factors, such as cultural differences, reporting variations, and, not least, widely varying dynamics within families—is a really lousy indicator of future performance, either individual or national.

Why then have parents, teachers, and policymakers continued to obsess about the amount of homework assigned at various grade levels? I believe there are two reasons. The first is simply that homework is an easy thing to argue about. Ten minutes? An hour? Reduced to a matter of duration, as opposed to quality or nuance, it's easy to stake out a position. More deeply, however, people argue about *how much* homework there should be because homework itself seems to be a given— so deeply ingrained as part of our standard but archaic educational model that inquiries into the subject never really get down to bedrock.

So then, let's circle back to our original question: How much homework is the right amount?

The answer is: No one knows. It all depends.

If that answer seems unsatisfying and deflating, it actually points the way to a very useful insight: The reason we can't come up with a meaningful answer is that we're asking the wrong question. We should be asking something far more basic. Not *how much* homework, but *why* homework in the first place?

Why are certain pedagogical tasks consigned to the classroom and the rigidly structured time increments of the school day, while others are pushed back into the looser hours of personal and family time?

Why do we assume that teachers' skills are best deployed in broadcasting information to an entire class, then sending kids home to work out problems on their own, often without the chance to ask questions or receive help? Given the pressures of fulfilling set curricula and meeting various governmental guidelines, it is often impossible to review or discuss homework assignments; how valuable is homework that doesn't get reviewed?

These are the kinds of questions we should be asking—questions that examine some of our longest-held educational habits and assumptions, and are therefore quite threatening to the educational establishment.

Let's start with a line of inquiry so deceptively simple that it seems to be a tautology, but in fact reveals some of the contradictions and misconceptions regarding homework: Why was homework designed to be done at home?

Different people will give you different answers. Some believe it was to teach students responsibility, accountability, and time management. Others would say that it encouraged students to learn independently. I am actually a fan of these two assertions.

Another line of reasoning is that homework was meant to involve parents in the process of their children's education. The ideal scenario—straight out of 1950s television, though the idea is actually older—was built around the idea of an intact nuclear family sitting around together in the evening. Susie and Johnny would have their schoolbooks open on the dining room table or the living room floor, while Dad, recently home from a nine-to-five job, smoked his pipe, read the paper, and was free to expound wisdom on almost any subject, and Mom, who'd been home most of the day, vacuuming and baking cookies, could chime in deferentially on questions that were not Dad's strong points. Whether this idyll ever really existed is open to discussion; in any event, certainly no one who cares about education should overlook the benefit of involving families in the schooling of their kids. But there are far better ways—as we'll see—to welcome parents into the learning process, especially given that the two-parent, one-earner household has by now become the exception rather than the rule.

For many if not most families, time together has become an increasingly rare and precious commodity. Moms work. Adults of both genders put in longer hours, endure longer commutes, travel on business. Kids confront an ever wider array of distractions and so-called social media whose net effect, ironically enough, is to make people *less* social, more head-down on their keyboards or keypads. Aside from that, as teaching modalities have evolved and more advanced subject matter has found its way into K-12 curricula, fewer parents are really equipped to help kids with their homework.

So then, is doing homework really the best use of time that families might otherwise spend just *being together*? Studies suggest otherwise. One large survey conducted by the University of Michigan concluded that the single strongest predictor of better achievement scores and fewer behavioral problems was not time spent on homework, but rather the frequency and duration of family meals.[11] If we think about it, this really shouldn't be surprising. When families actually sit down and talk—when parents and children exchange ideas and truly show an interest in each other—kids absorb values, motivation, self-esteem; in short, they grow in exactly those attributes and attitudes that will make them enthusiastic and attentive learners. This is more important than mere homework.

There is another unintended and undesirable side effect of homework as it is usually assigned and generally understood. Traditional homework is a driver of inequality, and in this regard it runs directly counter both to the stated aims of public education and to our sense of fairness. Insofar as parents can help with homework, moms and dads who are themselves well educated obviously have a huge advantage. Even when the homework help is indirect, households with books and families with a tradition of educational success have an unfair edge. Wealthier kids are less likely to be burdened with after-school jobs or chores that single parents—or exhausted parents—can't perform. In short, homework contributes to an unlevel playing field in which, educationally speaking, the rich get richer and the poor get poorer.

Given all these drawbacks, why has it been accepted as gospel for so long that homework is *necessary*?

The answer, I think, lies not in the perceived virtues of homework but rather in the clear deficiencies of what happens in the classroom. Homework *becomes* necessary because not enough learning happens during the school day. Why is there a shortage of learning during the hours specifically designed for it? Because the broadcast, one-pace-fits-all lecture—the technique that is at the very heart of our standard classroom model—turns out to be a highly inefficient way to teach and learn.

Flipping the Classroom

When I started posting video lessons on YouTube, it became clear that many students around the world were using them to learn outside of a formal classroom. What was more surprising was that I soon got letters and comments from teachers. Some were pointing their students to the videos as a supplemental tool. Others, however, were using them to rethink their classrooms altogether.

These teachers saw that I had already made available lectures that students could watch at their own time and pace. So the teachers decided to stop giving lectures themselves. Instead, they used scarce class time for the type of problem-solving more normally done as homework. Students could then watch the videos at home. This solved two problems at once.

As we've seen, students learn at different rates. Attention spans tend to max out at around fifteen minutes. Active learning creates more durable neural pathways than passive learning. Yet the passive in-class lecture—in which the entire class is expected to absorb information at the same rate, for fifty minutes or an hour, while sitting still and silent in their chairs—remains our dominant teaching mode. This results in the majority of students being lost or bored at any given time, even when there is a great lecturer.

They then go home and attempt to do homework, which raises another set of concerns. Generally, kids are asked to work in a vacuum. If they get stuck on a problem, there's nowhere to turn for help. Frustration—and often sleep deprivation—sets in. By the time class reconvenes, chances are the exact nature of the difficulty has been forgotten. Throughout this process, students get limited feedback on how well they are actually grasping the information. Until the unit exam, teachers too are left with little feedback on how well the students understand the topic. By then, however, gaps in student understanding cannot be fixed because the entire class has to move on to the next topic.

In the model that these teachers were using—lecture at home, "homework" in class—students had the benefit of having the teacher and their peers around when they were problem-solving. That way, difficulties or misconceptions were addressed as they were actually occurring. The teachers, rather than giving broadcast lectures, worked with individual students who needed help. Students who caught on faster assisted those who were struggling. Teachers also had the benefit of forming personal connections with students and getting real feedback on student comprehension. The use of technology had, somewhat ironically, made a traditionally passive classroom interactive and human.

Lectures at home—or, for that matter, on the bus, in the park, or interspersed with the in-class exercises—were also more productive. This kind of independent, on-demand learning was a much more active process than in-class lectures.

Students decided what they needed to watch and when. They could pause and repeat as necessary; they took responsibility for their own learning. A student could review basic concepts that they were embarrassed to ask about in front of their peers. If the current topic was intuitive, the student could learn more advanced topics or go outside and play. If parents choose to get involved as learning partners, they could; the video lessons were available to them as well as to their kids.

What about students who seldom did traditional homework? Wouldn't it be even more difficult to have them watch videos at home? After all, there was now nothing tangible that they had to show the next day in class. First, I believe that the primary reason why most students don't complete their homework is frustration. They don't understand the material and no one is there to help and give feedback. But some people might argue that there are students who are just plain not going to do any type of homework for lack of motivation or time. Even if this is the case, in my opinion it is far better to miss out on the lecture than the problem-solving. The lectures are gravy; the real meat of the learning occurs when peers are learning and teaching one another alongside the teacher.

Lectures done independently at a student's pace; problem-solving in class. This notion of "flipping the classroom" was around before Khan Academy existed and clearly wasn't my idea. However, the popularity of the Khan Academy video library seems to have pushed it into mainstream thinking. This association has been something of a double-edged sword. On one hand, I believe the flipped classroom is a simple but dramatic way to make classrooms more engaging for all involved.

On the other hand, it is just an optimization within a Prussian assembly-line model of education. Although it makes class time more interactive and lectures more independent, the "flipped classroom" still has students moving together in age-based cohorts at roughly the same pace, with snapshot exams that are used more to label students than address their weaknesses. As we'll see later in this book, technology now gives us the opportunity to go much, much further and fully liberate students' intellect and creativity from the bonds of the Prussian model.

The Economics of Schooling

Before moving on from this critique of our standard educational model, I would like to briefly address one more strange and paradoxical thing about it: It may not be working very well, but it certainly is expensive.

There are widely varying computations of what education actually costs. The methodologies for deriving the numbers are often tainted by competing ideologies, and so should be regarded with caution. But let's consider a couple of figures that seem pretty solid and tough to argue with. In the United States, for the school year 2008–2009 (the most recent year for which comparative numbers are available), the average cost per student for a single year of secondary public education was $10,499. To put this number in perspective, consider that it is larger than the entire per capita gross domestic product of Russia or Brazil. In New York, the state with the highest education costs, the figure was $18,126 per student, more than the per capita GDP of such wealthy nations as South Korea and Saudi Arabia.

Now, like everyone else involved in our education debates, I feel that money devoted to learning is money well spent—especially compared to the vast sums squandered on military contracting, farm subsidies, bridges to nowhere, and so forth. Still, waste in certain areas of our public life does not justify waste in others, and the sad truth is that a significant part of what we spend on education is just that—waste. We spend lavishly but not wisely. We obsess about *more* because we cannot envision or agree about *better*.

At roughly $10,000 per student per year, the average American school is spending $250,000–$300,000 per classroom of twenty-five to thirty students. Where is that money going? Arguably, most of it *should* be going to teachers; but that isn't how it works. Teachers' salaries are a relatively small part of the expenditure. If we generously put a teacher's salary and benefits at $100,000 per year—teachers in most of the country make far less—and the cost of maintaining a 1,000-square-foot classroom at $30,000 per year (a figure comparable to leasing high-end office space), we still have $120,000–$170,000 *for each classroom* to be spent on "other stuff." This other stuff includes things like well-paid administrators, security guards, and well-manicured football fields—none of which have a direct role in students' learning.

Clearly, teachers could and should be significantly better paid if some of the fat were trimmed from the bureaucracy and if more wisdom than tradition went into decisions about what expenses really drive learning. It's not the teachers' fault if superintendents and boards make unproductive choices; still, in the blame game that much of our education debate has become, teachers have come in for criticism that is often unfair or at least disproportionate to their role in the fiscal mess and the misallocation of resources.

In order to really address these problems, it's not enough to fix things on the margin: Add a day in the calendar here, change teacher compensation there. We can't just focus on things like student/teacher ratio. In regard to cost as well as standard classroom techniques, we need to question basic assumptions.

For example, student/teacher ratio is important. Obviously, the fewer students per teacher, the more attention each student will get. But isn't the student-to-valuable-time-with-the-teacher ratio more important? I have sat in eight-person college seminars where I never had a truly meaningful interaction with the professor; I have been in thirty-person classrooms where the teacher took a few minutes to work with me and mentor me directly on a regular basis.

Improving the student/teacher *time* ratio doesn't necessarily take money; it takes a willingness to rethink our classroom methods. If we move away from the broadcast lecture, students can have more of the teacher's one-to-one attention; good teachers will get to do more of what led them to teaching in the first place—helping kids learn.

Shifting the focus for a moment from public schools to private schools, it can be argued that if the money spent on public education in the United States and other wealthy nations is a necessary extravagance, the money lavished on elite private schools borders on the obscene. To send a child to a top-tier day school costs around $40,000 a year (or roughly $400,000 to $800,000 per year for a classroom of ten to twenty students). Boarding schools may charge more than $60,000. For affluent families in our megacompetitive culture, the tuition is often just a down payment. When the school day is done, the private tutors take over, sometimes charging as much as $500 per hour; it is not unheard of for parents to spend six figures a year, in addition to tuition, on a child's tutoring.[12] The tutoring these days goes well beyond the standard SAT test prep, and is sometimes tailored to specific courses at specific private schools. In an otherwise terrible job market, high-end tutoring has become a boutique growth industry.

But here's the good news. If the outsized and somewhat hysterical spending on private education is unhealthy and unsustainable, it's also completely unnecessary. First, most private schools do not show a discernible difference in results relative to public schools that cater to students with a similar demographic. Second, rigorous, high-quality, and personalized education can be delivered for far, far less money. It needn't be the sole prerogative of the wealthiest families in the wealthiest nations. This kind of education can and should be available to everyone.

What will make this goal attainable is the enlightened use of technology. Let me stress ENLIGHTENED use. Clearly, I believe that technology-enhanced teaching and learning is our best chance for an affordable and equitable educational future. But the key question is how the technology is used. It's not enough to put a bunch of computers and smartboards into classrooms. The idea is to integrate the technology into how we teach and learn; without meaningful and imaginative integration, technology in the classroom could turn out to be just one more very expensive gimmick.

Other educators, it should be pointed out, share my skepticism regarding the quick but shallow adoption of new classroom technologies. Duke University professor Cathy N. Davidson has written that "if you change the technology but not the method of learning, then you are throwing good money after bad practice.... [The iPad] is not a classroom learning tool unless you restructure the classroom.... The metrics, the methods, the goals and the assessments all need to change."[13]

Let's think a moment about those methods and those metrics. The dominant method in our traditional classrooms is still the broadcast lecture; one of the most cited metrics in our public debates is class size. But there's a disconnect between those things. If a teacher's main job is lecturing, what does it really matter how many students are in the room? Whatever the class size, how customized can instruction be when kids sit passively, taking notes, and the great majority of the teacher's time and energy is devoted to lesson plans, grading papers, and paperwork?

The promise of technology is to liberate teachers from those largely mechanical chores so that they have more time for human interactions. In many standard classrooms, teachers are so overburdened with mundane tasks that they are lucky to carve out 10 or 20 percent of class time to actually *be* with students— face-to-face, one-on-one, talking and listening. Imagine what could happen if that figure went to 90 or 100 percent of class time. The student-to-time-with-the teacher ratio would improve by a factor of five or ten. And this is the metric we should care about.

Does all this sound utopian? Purely theoretical? It's neither. In actual fact, this liberated style of teaching is already being deployed in the real world. In the next part of our book, we will examine how this came to be and how it seems to be working.

PART 3

Into the Real World

Theory versus Practice

If complaining about the status quo is easy, theorizing about how things ought to be is not much harder. Academic papers pile up, advocating this or that approach—more grading, less grading; more testing, less testing. In education as in every other field, there are fads and fashions. Looking at it positively, these fads sometimes point the way to true innovation. But other times they prove to be overly generalized dead ends, costly in terms of both money and wasted time.

As an example of this, consider the hypothesis that people have different "learning styles." Around thirty years ago, it was proposed that some people are primarily "verbal learners" while others are mainly "visual learners." On the face of it, this seemed a reasonable idea. Some people, after all, seem better with names than with faces, and vice versa. Confronted with a user's manual for some new device, some people will read the text while others will go straight to the diagrams. Ergo, visual learning versus verbal learning. This seemingly commonsensical observation gained favor and thereby "created a thriving commercial market amongst researchers, educators, and the general public."[1] Separate exercises and even textbooks were devised for each purported learning style. Shiny new teacher's guides were printed up and put on sale to willing school districts. As many as seventy-one different learning styles had been suggested.

There were only two problems with the "learning styles" theory. The first was that it really didn't hold water. In 2009, a report published in *Psychological Science in the Public Interest* reviewed the major studies that had suggested that people have different learning styles. The great majority of studies didn't meet the minimum standards to be scientifically valid. The few that did seem valid—that rigorously examined whether instructing people in their purported learning style really improved their results—seemed to contradict the thesis. Teaching according to "learning styles" had no discernible effect.

The second problem was that given the very laborious chores of designing research studies, compiling sufficient data, analyzing the data, and publishing the results, it took *thirty years* to find this out. Who knows how much money and time—both teachers' and students'—was squandered during that three-decade experiment.

While thirty years seems egregious, some significant time lag is probably unavoidable when it comes to testing new approaches, and at the very least this should make us cautious when a promising learning theory comes along—especially if it purports to be a universal theory. The human brain is so complex that we should never become dogmatic about a particular approach being the best way for everyone.

In medicine, I can give a real pill of a certain drug to one group of patients and a sugar pill—the placebo—to another group. After a few months or years of this, I can then see whether the group taking the real pill had a statistically significant improvement in their health versus the placebo group. If this happened, I can generalize that the particular drug would be appropriate for patients like those in the test groups. What I can't do is *overgeneralize*. I can't posit that the same drug would necessarily work for different populations of patients, still less patients with different diseases.

In fields like education, however, this tendency to overgeneralize is a constant danger.

Say I want to figure out the best way to make educational materials, maybe science videos. My theory is that videos that show a dialog between a student and a professor will be more effective than just the lecturer alone. I get two sets of videos produced that cover the same topic—say Newton's laws—in both styles. I then randomly assign students to watch either set of videos and give them an assessment. Say I find that the students who watched the dialog version perform significantly better, enough of a difference that it would be unlikely due to chance alone. I therefore publish a paper titled "Dialog More Effective Than Lectures When Teaching Science Through Videos."

Now, would it be appropriate to make this generalization? Assuming the same professor was in both videos, maybe he in particular is more effective at dialog than lectures. Maybe another professor might have been better in the lecture style. Maybe the professor was uniformly mediocre in both, but the dialog videos had the benefit of a student with the knack for asking the right questions and summarizing the professor's words. Maybe getting that student to make pure lectures would be even better because they would be unfettered by the professor. Perhaps the results would have been different had the topic been relativity or if the lecture videos didn't show the professor's face or if a different type of assessment were used.

The point is that the only conclusion that can responsibly be made from this experiment is that the particular videos that happened to be made in the dialog style performed better than the particular videos made in the lecture style for that particular topic and according to that particular assessment. It says nothing about whether in general all science videos should be in the dialog style.

Now, if you are properly skeptical of everything I am saying, a thought should be nagging you right now: Sal has been writing this entire book about ways to improve education, and now he is saying that it is irresponsible to make sweeping statements about the best way to educate. The difference is in how the arguments are made and how general the statements are. I am arguing for a particular set of practices that are already showing results with many students and can be tested and refined with many others; I'm not arguing for a generalized theory.

I am not saying that "science" has proven that *any* self-paced videos and exercises coupled with any in-class projects will be better than *any* 300-person lecture. In fact, I think that statement is outright false. What I am saying is that although we are in the early stages of this adventure, we are seeing compelling evidence—both anecdotal and statistical—that particular types of practices with videos and software seem to be resonating with particular students and teachers. I really don't know if it is the absolute best way to reach every student—frankly, there probably are students who might do better in the more passive Prussian model. What we want to do is to use the traction and data we have to continue to repeatedly refine and test our particular content and software and make it as effective as possible for as many people as possible.

My personal philosophy is to do what makes sense and not try to confirm a dogmatic bias with pseudoscience. It is grounded in using data to iteratively refine an educational experience without attempting to make sweeping statements about how the unimaginably complex human mind always works. Use video-based lectures for certain contexts; use live dialogs, when possible, for others. Use projects when appropriate and traditional problem sets when appropriate. Focus both on what students need to prove to the world through assessments and on what students actually need to *know* in the real world. Focus on the pure and the thought-provoking as well as on the practical. Why restrict oneself to one or the other? The old answer was that there wasn't enough time to do both. Thanks to technology, that excuse no longer applies. Nor does education need to be hostage to any dogmatic theory. We can now craft more *particular and individual* solutions than ever before, thanks to the availability of data from millions of students on a daily basis.

This is not theory and this is not the future. It's happening in the real world and it's happening now.

The Khan Academy
Software

Let's do a quick rewind to 2004 to revisit how all this began.

Back then I still had my day job at the hedge fund. The Khan Academy, as well as the YouTube videos that have come to be its most visible feature, was far off in the future. I was just a guy who did a little private tutoring by telephone.

Right from the start, I was troubled, even shocked, to realize that most of my tutees—even though they were generally motivated and "successful" students—had only a very shaky grasp of core material, especially in math. There were many basic concepts that they sort of half understood. They might, for example, be able to describe what a prime number was (a number divisible only by itself and 1), but not explain how that concept related to the more general idea of least common multiples. In brief, the formulas were there, the rote stuff had been memorized, but the connections were missing. The intuitive leaps had not been made. Why not? Chances are that the material had been gone over too quickly and shallowly in class, with related concepts ghettoized by their artificial division into units. The bottom line was that kids didn't really know *math*; they knew certain words and processes that *described* math.

This half-understanding had consequences that showed up very quickly during the one-to-one tutoring sessions. In response to even the simplest questions, students tended to give very tentative answers—answers that sounded like guesses even when they weren't. It seemed to me there were two reasons for this lack of assertiveness. The first was that because the students' grasp of core material stopped short of true *conceptual* understanding, they were seldom quite sure exactly what was being asked or which conceptual tool should be used to solve the problem. To offer a rough analogy, it was as if they'd been taught, in two different lessons, how to use a hammer and how to use a screwdriver. Told to hammer, they could hammer. Told to put in a screw, they could use a screwdriver. But told to build a shelf, they'd be paralyzed even though it was just a combination of concepts that they should have learned.

The second issue was simple confidence. The kids gave wishy-washy answers because they knew deep down that they were bluffing. This, of course, was not their fault; their previous education had been of the Swiss cheese sort and had left them teetering on an inadequate foundation.

In terms of the live tutoring sessions, these deficiencies in core understanding became a big headache. Identifying and remediating each student's particular gaps would have been hugely time-consuming, and would have left little time or energy to move on to more advanced concepts. The process, I imagine, would also have been painful and humiliating for the student. *Okay, tell me what else you don't know.*

So with the goal of creating a time-efficient way to help repair my tutees' educational gaps, I wrote some very simple software to generate math problems. To be sure, this early software was pretty basic. All it did was spit out random problems on various topics such as adding and subtracting negative numbers or working with simple exponents. Students could work on as many of these problems as they needed to, until they felt they had a concept nailed. If they didn't know how to do a particular problem, the software would show steps for coming to the right answers.

But the primitive problem-generating software still left a number of things unaddressed. My tutees could work as many exercises as they chose to, but I, the tutor, had no real information on the process. So I added a database that allowed me to track how many problems each student got right or wrong, how much time they spent, even the time of day when they were working. At first I thought of this as a mere convenience, an efficient way of keeping tabs. Only gradually did the full potential usefulness of this feedback system occur to me; by expanding and refining the feedback I could begin to understand not only *what* my students were learning but *how* they were learning. In terms of real-world results, this struck me as important.

For example, did students spend more time on problems they got right or on problems they got wrong? Did they grind their way through to solutions (by logical steps), or see answers in a flash (by pattern recognition)? Were the mistakes just carelessness or the result of an inability to complete a strand of connections? What happened when a student truly "got" a concept?

Did this happen gradually by seeing a repetition of examples, or in a sudden *Aha* moment? What happened when students did a bunch of problems focusing on one concept rather than a mixed hodgepodge of problems focused on many types of concepts?

Working with my small roster of tutees, I was fascinated by the variations in the data on these sorts of questions about the *how* of learning. As we shall see, this accumulated data would over time become a valuable resource for teachers, administrators, and educational researchers.

In the meantime, however, I had more immediate difficulties to solve. As my number of students grew, I came closer and closer to hitting a wall that millions of teachers have hit before me when attempting to personalize instruction. How could I manage twenty or thirty students working on different subjects, at different grade levels, each at his or her own pace? How could I keep track of who needed what and who was ready to advance to more challenging material?

Fortunately, this kind of information management is exactly what computers are good at. So the next step in the refinement of the software was to devise a hierarchy or web of concepts—the "knowledge map" we've already seen—so that the system itself could advise students what to work on next. Once they'd mastered the addition and subtraction of fractions, for example, they could move on to simple linear equations. Having the software hand out the "assignments" left me free to do the essentially human parts of the job—the actual mentoring and tutoring.

But this raised an absolutely crucial question: How could

I determine when a student was ready to advance? How would I define "mastery" of a given concept? This proved to be a philosophical as well as a practical question.

One possibility was to use the traditional percentage of right answers that most exams defined as "passing." But this just didn't feel right. In a traditional classroom, you could pass with 70 percent—which meant there was almost one-third of the material that you didn't know. I could arbitrarily raise my own passing grade to 80 or 85 or 90 percent, but this seemed rather lazy and beside the point. As we've seen, even a 95 percent grasp of basic concepts led to difficulties later on, so why settle for that?

The issue, I eventually realized, came down not to some numerical target but to a much more human consideration: expectations. What level of application and understanding should we expect from our students? In turn, what sort of messages are we sending by way of our expectations and the standards they imply? My gut feeling was that in general the expectations of teachers and educators are far too low, and, further, that there is something condescending and contagious in this attitude. Kids come to doubt their own abilities when they sense that the bar is being set so low. Or they develop the corrosive and limiting belief that good enough is good enough.

I eventually formed the conviction that my cousins—and all students—needed higher expectations to be placed on them. Eighty or 90 percent is okay, but I wanted them to work on things until they could get ten right answers in a row. That may sound radical or overidealistic or just too difficult, but I would argue that it was the only simple standard that was truly respectful of both the subject matter and the students. (We have refined the scoring details a good bit since then, but the basic philosophy hasn't changed.) It's demanding, yes. But it doesn't set students up to fail; it sets them up to succeed—because they can keep trying until they reach this high standard.

I happen to believe that every student, given the tools and the help that he or she needs, can reach this level of proficiency in basic math and science. I also believe it is a disservice to allow students to advance *without* this level of proficiency, because they'll fall on their faces sometime later.

With those core beliefs in place, I still had the practical question of how to cultivate and measure 100 percent proficiency. Typically, I had no grand theory about this; I just decided to try the heuristic of ten-in-a-row. My reasoning was that if students could correctly solve ten consecutive problems on a given subject, it was a good indication that they truly understood the underlying concept. Lucky guesses would fall short, as would mere "plug-ins." Admittedly, ten was an arbitrary number of solutions to shoot for; I might have gone with eight or twelve or whatever, and different concepts probably require a different number. But insisting on a particular number of right answers gave students something to aim at. If they fell short, they could always go back and review. If they needed more problems to try, the software would create them.

Best of all, when students nailed ten problems in a row—a feat that generally seemed quite daunting at the start—they really felt that they'd accomplished something. Their confidence and self-esteem had been boosted, and they looked forward to the challenge of the next, more difficult concept.

The Leap to a Real Classroom

Let's now jump to early 2007.

As of then, several thousand students were using the Khan Academy videos that had recently begun to be posted on YouTube. Of those thousands, some hundreds were also availing themselves of the problem-generating capability of the site. Clearly, the Academy was growing beyond my handful of tutees; word of mouth was spreading and the exponential viral growth was not too far off in the future. This was gratifying, of course, but there was also something surreal about it. I was accustomed to having a personal relationship with everyone I tutored. Now, except for my cousins and family friends, I didn't really know my students, except through their work and occasional emails; I felt a little bit like a doctor who analyzes lab results but doesn't see patients.

I hadn't yet had the privilege and the challenge of interfacing with real-world classroom teachers and students. The problem-generating software and the rather basic feedback loop worked well enough for me; would they work for anybody else? What refinements or criticisms would be offered by the professionals who were actually in the trenches? Would teachers embrace the online video concept or feel threatened by it? Would the ideas I had been experimenting with be most productively used as a full curriculum or an add-on?

Eager to see firsthand how students interacted with the software and the videos, I was excited when, through a friend, I was introduced to a teacher who was helping to run a summer program here in the Bay Area. The program is known as Peninsula Bridge, and its mandate is to provide educational opportunity to motivated middle-school kids from underresourced schools and neighborhoods; toward this end, a number of the Bay Area's most prestigious private schools donate the use of their facilities. Once a student is accepted, he or she is invited, tuition-free, to attend a summer session.

I was eager to participate, but first I had to convince the faculty and the board that I had something to offer. I have to admit that this "audition" made me nervous. This was odd. In my work at the hedge fund I routinely went, unfazed, into meetings with CEOs and CFOs of major corporations; I breezed through discussions regarding investment choices where tens of millions of dollars (and possibly my job) were at stake. Now I was walking into very informal meetings with like-minded and generous-spirited people, and I was as jumpy as a teenager on his very first date.

My first conversation was with a woman named Ryanne Saddler, a history teacher and the summer site director at the Castilleja School, one of the institutions that lent its campus to Peninsula Bridge. I was so excited to have access to an actual member of the education establishment that I talked a mile a minute as I laid out the basics of what I had been working on—the videos, the self-paced exercises, the knowledge map, the feedback dashboard. Ryanne seemed to like what she heard, but since she herself was not a math teacher she suggested I do my dog-and-pony show in a meeting with the full board. I readily agreed, and as we were parting, Ryanne casually said, "This will all work on Macs, right?"

"Of course!" I said confidently.

This was a fib. I didn't own a Mac and I had no idea if my software would run on one. I went straight to the local computer store, bought a MacBook, and then pulled an all-nighter, hacking my way through to make everything—well, *mostly* everything—compatible.

If this was a somewhat shaky beginning to my relationship with real-world education, the omens soon got even worse. My meeting with the board was scheduled for March 15. By coincidence—or cruel fate—this was also the date on which my domain name, khanacademy.org, came up for renewal. Unbeknownst to me, the credit card I had left on file with the domain host had expired. And so as a gentle reminder that I owed them $12, the hosting company shut down the site. No warning, no grace period. On what was up to then the most important morning of the Academy's young existence.

The realization that the site was down had a strange effect on me; it made me very calm. Before that, I'd been a nervous wreck, wondering what gave me the gall to believe I could change the way education happens with my rather rustic, handcrafted videos and software. Now I realized that I had no chance. *A guy comes to show off his website, except that he has no website. What a loser!* Accepting defeat before I even started, I went into the meeting equipped with an old-fashioned slide-show and the videos that were on YouTube.

At Ryanne's suggestion, I showed a video that I had done on "Basic Addition," which I felt was clumsily made, and possibly even cheesy—I still cringe when I hear my own voice. Luckily, everyone else seemed mildly entertained to hear a grown man count avocados while seeing shaky handwritten text appear on a virtual blackboard. They concluded that the Academy might be of real use in fulfilling their goal of getting kids ready to face algebra. They seemed as excited as I was to give it a try.

It turned out that Peninsula Bridge used the video lessons and software at three of its campuses that summer. Some of the ground rules were clear. The Academy would be used in addition to, not in place of, a traditional math curriculum. The videos would only be used during "computer time," a slot that was shared with learning other tools such as Adobe Photoshop and Illustrator. Even within this structure, however, there were some important decisions to be made; the decisions, in turn, transformed the Peninsula Bridge experience into a fascinating and in some ways surprising test case.

The first decision was the question of *where* in math the kids should start. The Academy math curriculum began, literally, with 1 + 1 = 2. But the campers were mainly sixth to eighth graders. True, most of them had serious gaps in their under-standing of math and many were working below their grade level. Still, wouldn't it be a bit insulting and a waste of time to start them with basic addition? I thought so, and so I proposed beginning at what would normally be considered fifth-grade material, in order to allow for some review. To my surprise, however, two of the three teachers who were actually implementing the plan said they preferred to start at the very beginning. Since the classes had been randomly chosen, we thereby ended up with a small but classic controlled experiment.

The first assumption to be challenged was that middle-school students would find basic arithmetic far too easy. Among the groups that had started with 1 + 1, most of the kids, as expected, rocketed through the early concepts. But some didn't. A few got stuck on things as fundamental as two-digit subtraction problems. Some had clearly never learned their multiplication tables. Others were lacking basic skills regarding fractions or division. I stress that these were motivated and intelligent kids. But for whatever reason, the Swiss cheese gaps in their learning had started creeping in at a distressingly early stage, and until those gaps were repaired they had little chance of mastering algebra and beyond.

The good news, however, is that once identified, those gaps *could* be repaired, and that when the shaky foundation had been rebuilt, the kids were able to advance quite smoothly.

This was in vivid and unexpected contrast to the group that had started at the fifth-grade level. Since they'd begun with such a big head start, I assumed that by the end of the six-week program they would be working on far more advanced concepts than the other group. In fact just the opposite happened. As in the classic story of the tortoise and the hare, the 1 + 1 group plodded and plodded and eventually passed them right by. Some of the students in the "head start" group, on the other hand, hit a wall and just couldn't seem to progress. There were sixth- and seventh-grade concepts that they simply couldn't seem to master, presumably because of gaps in *earlier* concepts. In comparing the performance of the two groups, the conclusion seemed abundantly clear: Nearly all the students needed some degree of remediation, and *the time spent on finding and fixing the gaps turned out both to save time and deepen learning in the longer term.*

But how did we discover where the gaps were, how big a hurdle they posed, and when they'd been adequately filled in?

As I've mentioned, I had already designed a pretty basic database that allowed me to keep track of the progress of my own tutees. But now I was working with experienced classroom teachers who pointed the way to significant refinements in the feedback system. A few days into the camp schedule, one of these teachers, Christine Hemiup, emailed me to say that while the existing functionality was spiffy, what she really needed was a simple way to identify when students were "stuck."

This, in turn, led to a meditation on the concept of "stuckness." Learning, after all, always entails a degree of being "stuck," if only for a moment, on the cusp between what one doesn't know and what one has come to understand. So I realized that, as in the case of mastery, I would have to come up with a somewhat arbitrary heuristic for defining "stuckness." I settled on this: If a student attempted fifty problems and at no point got ten in a row right, then he or she was "stuck." (This heuristic has by now been refined using fairly advanced techniques, but the general idea is the same—figure out who could most use help from the teacher or another student.)

This rough definition of "stuckness" served well enough as a framework, but still left the question of how best to get the information to the teacher. Christine suggested a daily spreadsheet with each student represented by a row, and each concept pictured as a column. At every intersection of student and concept there would be a "cell," in which we could put information as to how many problems had been worked, the number right or wrong, the longest streak, and time spent. The spreadsheet would provide a simple and graphic account of who was stuck and where.

As it turned out, the feedback spreadsheet was much more than a tidy graphic feature; it fundamentally altered the dynamic of the classroom. Once again, *the use of technology made the classroom more human* by facilitating one-on-one interactions; by letting the teacher know who needed her attention most. Even better, a student who had already mastered a particular concept could be paired with one who was struggling. Or two students, stuck in the same place, could work together to get past their common hurdle. In all of these instances, the clear emphasis would be on quality, helping interactions.

Before leaving this account of the Peninsula Bridge experience, I'd like to mention one anecdotal outcome that I found particularly interesting and hopeful. In the traditional model of education we've inherited from the Prussians, students are moved together in cohorts. Because it appears that—in a traditional classroom—the spread between the fastest and slowest students grows over time, putting them all in one class cohort eventually makes it exceedingly difficult to avoid either completely boring the fast students or completely losing the slow ones. Most school systems address this by "tracking" students. This means putting the "fastest" students in "advanced" or "gifted" classes, the average students in "average" classes, and the slowest students into "remedial" classes. It seems logical... except for the fact that it creates a somewhat permanent intellectual and social division between students.

The assessments that decide the fates of these students can also be somewhat arbitrary in their timing and in what they say about the potential of the student. So I was very curious to see if there were any data from the camp that showed that if "slow" students have the opportunity to work at their own pace and build a strong foundation, they could become "advanced" or "fast." I did a database query for students who, at the start of the program, seriously lagged their peers—and would therefore have probably been tracked "slow" by placement exams—but who then turned out to be among the top performers.

In one class of only thirty students, I found three who had started the six-week program significantly below average and finished it significantly *above* average. (For the statistically minded, I measured this by comparing the number of concepts mastered by each student against the average number completed by the group, during the first and last weeks of the program. I then focused on those who at the start of camp were at least one standard deviation below the norm, and by the end were at least one standard deviation above it.) In plain English, what this admittedly tiny sample suggested was that fully 10 percent of the kids might have been tracked as slow, and treated accordingly, when they were fully capable of doing very well in math.

There was one seventh-grade girl—I'll call her Marcela—whose results were especially striking. At the start of camp, Marcela was among the least advanced of the students, and during the first half of the summer session her progress was among the slowest; she was working through roughly half as many concepts as the average student. In particular, she was spending an inordinate amount of time wrestling with the concepts of adding and subtracting negative numbers; she was about as stuck as stuck could get. Then something clicked. I don't know exactly how it happened, and neither did her classroom teacher; that's part of the wonderful mystery of human intelligence. She had one of those *Aha* moments, and from then on she progressed faster than nearly anyone else in the class. At the end of the program, she was the second most advanced of all the students. Moreover, she was showing mathematical intuitions that hinted at a genuine gift; she ended up breezing through complex topics that most of her peers—even the ones that thought they were "good" at math—struggled with.

At the close of camp, we held a little awards ceremony. I had the pleasure of presenting prizes to a few of the kids, Marcela among them. She was very shy and—until that summer—very short on confidence, and when I told her she'd become a rock star, she managed just the smallest smile and a quick nod. That was more than enough to make my day.

Fun and Games

In terms of my own learning curve in the realities of education, the Peninsula Bridge experience was both thrilling and liberating. When I was recording the video lessons to post on YouTube, remember, I was sitting all by myself in a glorified closet. Now I was dealing with flesh-and-blood kids whom I enjoyed and rooted for, and classroom teachers whose wisdom and commitment I greatly admired. My appetite for camps and classrooms had been whetted, and during the next couple of summers, starting in 2009, I codesigned and co-ran, with an aerospace engineer named Aragon Burlingham, what I thought of as an experiment in hands-on learning. As I still had my hedge fund job during the first of these summers, I used almost all my vacation time to be at the camp, and I didn't mind at all. I was having a blast.

As I hope is clear by now, it was never my vision that watching computer videos and working out problems should comprise a kid's entire education. Quite the contrary. My hope was to make education more efficient, to help kids master basic concepts in fewer hours so that more time would be left for *other* kinds of learning. Learning by doing. Learning by having productive, mind-expanding fun. Call it stealth learning. Summer camp seemed a perfect testing ground for these other aspects of education.

Our camps were therefore largely built with an emphasis on real projects that would in turn illustrate underlying principles. If that sounds a little dry and abstract, let me bring it home with a vivid example. Much of our time at the camps was spent in building robots. In one project, students were tasked with designing—using programmable Legos with sophisticated touch, light, and infrared sensors—tabletop sumo wrestlers. These robots needed to detect their opponent robot (or robots) and push them off the table. It was a simple game with open-ended opportunities for complexity.

Some students built smart and nimble robots that tried to trick their opponents into driving themselves off the tables. Others optimized for traction or torque. Most importantly, the kids repeatedly built, tested, and refined their unique concepts.

Another camp activity that proved fertile ground for learning was a variation on the familiar board game Risk. We played a variation called "Paranoia Risk" with the wrinkle that each player could only win by specifically eliminating one other randomly assigned player. You knew who you were supposed to destroy; you *didn't* know who was trying to destroy you. Hence the paranoia. You had to infer the malice from the other players' actions. Then you had to decide when it was better to simply pursue your own immediate interests, as opposed to playing defense vis-à-vis your predator or offense against your prey.

While the six players were implicitly learning about psychology, game theory, and probability directly through the game, the other twenty students were trading on the outcome, and thereby understanding how information and emotion drives markets. Each of the nonplayers was given $500 in fake money and six pieces of colored construction paper—one for each color of the players on the gameboard—at the start of the game. The rule was that the paper representing an eliminated player would be worth zero, while the paper representing a winning competitor would be worth $100. So, as you would expect, the price of each player's "stock" went up or down in accordance with the ebb and flow of the game; if someone was willing to pay $60 for the red paper, he was telling the market that he believed red had a 60 percent chance of winning (60 percent × $100 = $60). Without knowing it, students were gaining deep intuitions about probability, expected value, and modeling unpredictable phenomena. At one point, a few "securities" were trading above $100—more than they could possibly return. This was a great discussion point after the game when we talked about "irrational exuberance."

Since no summer camp experience is complete without exhausting both the mind and body, we played a game called "critical mass freeze tag." In regular freeze tag one student attempts to freeze the others in place by touching them. They can be unfrozen by other students who haven't been frozen yet. In our variation, we experimented to see the number of freezers and the size of the playing field we needed to be able to freeze everyone. Again, this was stealth learning in action. The kids thought they were playing tag; they didn't realize until later that they were getting a deeper intuition for how complex systems work.

These summer camps—both Peninsula Bridge and the ones I ran with Aragon—were enriching experiences and had a validity all their own. At the same time, however, I was keenly aware that if Khan Academy was to be seen as a legitimate option for classroom education, it would have to prove its value as part of a formal curriculum during an actual school year. So I was thrilled—though of course nervous as usual—when the opportunity came along to do exactly that.

Taking the Plunge

By early 2009, the Khan Academy was starting to take on a life of its own. Tens of thousands of students were using it every day and I was spending every ounce of my free time to work on it. Actually I was even spending a little of my nonfree time. I tried my best to focus on my day job, but my heart was becoming fully invested with the potential of what the Khan Academy might be.

To make things more difficult for me, I got a random email one day from a gentleman named Jeremiah "Jerry" Hennessy. He was the cofounder of a major restaurant chain—BJ's Restaurants—who had also become a user of my videos after looking for ways to help his son with chemistry. He wanted to chat with me about what I was doing with the Khan Academy.

By this time I had already been approached by several entrepreneurs trying to convince me to turn my videos into a for-profit business, and I assumed that Jerry was just another one of these. It turned out that his message was just the opposite. He was convinced, even more so than I was at that juncture, that I was wasting my time as a hedge fund guy and that Khan Academy could help change the world as a not-for-profit. I was flattered by his confidence, of course, but tried not to take it too seriously. My son had just been born, my wife was still in training; it seemed irresponsible even to consider quitting my job.

Jerry understood this and didn't pressure me too much. But he'd sown a seed of possibility in my mind. As the year progressed, I began talking to him more and more frequently. By the summer of 2009, I'd begun to seriously consider the possibility.

By this point, tens of thousands of students were watching the videos on a regular basis. The software I wrote for my cousins had become so popular via word-of-mouth that it was making my $50-a-month web host crash; I actually had to stop new users from signing up just so the old ones could have a barely usable experience. Frankly, the possibilities surrounding the Khan Academy were so exciting that I had trouble doing my day job properly.

So I started to chat with my wife, Umaima, about quitting the hedge fund and doing the Academy full-time. We had enough savings for a solid down payment on a decent house in Silicon Valley, but not much more. My wife was bringing in a little money from her salary as a training rheumatologist. Still, the thought of giving up a regular paycheck was scary. Both Umaima and I had come from single-mother households whose earnings were slightly above the poverty line in a good year; neither of us was eager to revisit the financial austerity of our childhoods. So I was still wavering.

Then, in one week in August, two powerful things happened. The first was that the Khan Academy was chosen to be a finalist for a major award given by the Technology Museum of San Jose. The second was an email I received via YouTube.

It was from a student who wanted to tell me that where he'd come from, "blacks [were] not welcomed with open arms into schools." As a kid he'd been "force fed medication to keep me from talking [then] chastised for not speaking out when called on." With sorrow rather than anger, he said that "no teacher has ever done me any good." Determined to give him a chance at a quality education, his family saved enough money to move to a less prejudiced community, but still, he wrote, "without a real mastery of elementary math I was slow to progress."

The young man had made it to college, though he was still playing catch-up at the start. He wanted me to know that he'd "spent the entire summer on your YouTube page...and I just wanted to thank you for everything you are doing....Last week I tested for a math placement exam and I am now in Honors Math 200....I can say without any doubt that you have changed my life and the lives of everyone in my family."

Wow. People working at hedge funds are not used to getting letters like that. Between that email, the potential award from the museum, Jerry's prodding, and my wife's blessings, I decided to take the plunge. I figured I would be able to convince someone that the Khan Academy was a cause worth supporting and confidently told my wife that I would go back to a regular job if this didn't happen within a year.

In retrospect, I was unbelievably naïve. Despite already having more views on YouTube than MIT OpenCourseWare and Stanford combined, the Khan Academy was still a one-person operation run out of a closet. I had no experience running or raising money for a not-for-profit. Most discouragingly, the few foundations willing to talk to me were afraid to support something that no one else had. I can't tell you how many times I heard, "Well this sounds exciting, but how come no one else has given you money?"

The stress began to build by the fourth month—nothing like burning $5,000 a month out of savings while having a toddler in the house to put strain on a marriage. The first sign of hope came when I was invited to meet some folks at Google in January 2010. Apparently many of the senior engineers and executives had been using Khan Academy with their kids and wanted to hear more about it.

That first meeting had about ten people in it. I had prepared some laminated slides (I called them my presentation placemats) that showed them screenshots of what I had built, testimonials from users, and data from the Peninsula Bridge Program. I told them that I thought we could build a free virtual school for the world, one with instruction, practice, feedback. We also talked about how we could use the data I was collecting to fine-tune the experience. Everyone seemed very sympathetic to what I was doing, but I still didn't have any real indication that this would lead to anything.

After a few weeks, they invited me for a second meeting. Now things became interesting. They asked me to write a proposal for what I would do with $2 million; nothing too involved; two pages would do. A million dollars per page; not bad. Keep in mind that up to this point I had spent a grand total of about $2,000 on the Khan Academy.

I spent the night writing and rewriting an outline of how I

would go about hiring an engineering team to build out the software, how many videos I could produce in a year, and how many students we could reach in five or ten years. I sent it in and waited. I got a few assurances over the next few months that they were seriously looking at my proposal, but by this time I had become too cynical about the foundation world to expect anything.

Within a few months, I began updating my résumé; I'd realized I had less tolerance for digging into my savings than I thought. I wasn't even sure if I could find a job in finance anymore—after all, most employers weren't used to hiring people who'd quit their jobs to make YouTube videos for a year.

Then in April, I got another unexpected and providential email. The subject line was "I am a big fan," so of course I opened it at once! A woman whose name I did not immediately recognize was asking for an address where she could send the Academy a donation.

In itself this was not so unusual. Many people had already donated $5, $10, and even $100 at a time over PayPal. But this time a check for $10,000 arrived in the mail. The sender was named Ann Doerr. After a little frantic web research, I realized that Ann was the wife of famed venture capitalist John Doerr. I sent her an email thanking her for her generous support, and she wrote back suggesting we have lunch.

We agreed to meet in May in downtown Palo Alto. Ann arrived on a green-blue bicycle. We talked about what Khan Academy could be. When Ann asked how I was supporting myself and my family, I answered, trying not to sound too desperate, "I'm not; we're living off of savings." She nodded and we each went our way.

About twenty minutes later, I got a text message as I was parking in my driveway. It was from Ann: *You need to support yourself. I am sending a check for $100,000 right now.*

I almost crashed into the garage door.

Ann's text message was the beginning of a surreal series of events. Two months later, Aragon and I were running our little one-week summer camp for the second year. One afternoon, while I had twenty kids working on one of our crazy projects, I got a text message from Ann. Actually I got several from her in a row. They read something like:

At Aspen . . . hundreds of people in audience

Bill Gates onstage, talking about you

Good day wife let you quit job

What were these haiku really saying? Maybe these messages were meant for someone else? Maybe they were some type of prank? I booted a student off the computer nearest me and began to search for confirmation.

Sure enough, people were already blogging and tweeting about it. Bill Gates was onstage at the Aspen Ideas Festival talking about how he was a fan of Khan Academy and was using it for his own learning and for his kids. My mind immediately pictured all the half-ass videos I had made for my cousins, where my son is screaming in the background or I'm trying to cram in a concept before my wife comes home from work. Did Bill Gates really watch those?

The next few days were strange. I had eventually found video footage of the event; I knew it had really happened. But what was I to do next? Call him? It's not like Bill Gates was listed in the phone book.

After about a week, I got an email followed by a phone call from Gates's chief of staff. He told me that if I had some time available, Bill would like to fly me to Seattle to meet and see how he could support the Khan Academy. I was staring at my calendar as he was asking my availability; it was completely blank for the next month. Sitting in my closet and trying to sound as cool as possible, I said, "Sure, I think I could squeeze something in."

The meeting happened on August 22 at Bill's offices in Kirkland, Washington; they overlooked the water and were somewhat nicer than my closet. I was waiting in a conference room—with the now overused presentation placemats in hand—with several other people from the Gates Foundation. I think I was visibly nervous, so they reassured me that "Bill is just another human being; he's completely cool." This relaxed me a bit and I started to get a little chatty. After a few minutes, all of a sudden, everyone in the room began to look a bit more serious than they had thirty seconds before. Bill Gates had walked in and was standing behind me. Yeah, just another human being.

I jolted up, shook his hand, and said, "Um...nice to meet you." He sat down and then everyone kind of just waited.

Realizing that this was my cue, I spent the next fifteen minutes talking about what I thought the Khan Academy could do and how we would do it. Bill politely nodded throughout. I frankly didn't even know what I was saying. Twenty percent of my brain was doing the talking. The other 80 percent kept thinking, "Do you realize that you are talking to Bill Gates? Right there next to you at the table! BILL GATES! Look, it's Bill Gates! You better not screw this up! Don't even THINK about cracking any of your stupid jokes!"

He asked me a few questions and then said simply, "This is great."

Two days later, an article about the Khan Academy came out in *Fortune* magazine. It was titled "Bill Gates' Favorite Teacher." I had talked to the author, David Kaplan, a few weeks prior and knew that he had also talked to Gates, but still, that headline was unreal. The article made my mother cry—I think it was the first time she wasn't completely annoyed that I hadn't gone to medical school.

By September, it became clear that the Gates Foundation would fund the Khan Academy with a $1.5 million grant so that we could get office space and hire a team of five people; they later gave another $4 million to support other projects. Google also announced that it was awarding $2 million to the Khan Academy to further build out our exercise library and to translate our content into the ten most spoken world languages. This was part of their Project 10^100, whose goal was to fund five ideas to change the world, selected from 150,000 submissions. It seemed that it was time for me to come out of the closet.

The Los Altos Experiment

With some of the funding in place and some of the immediate financial pressures laid to rest, I was finally free to return to job one: education.

In September 2010, I'd been introduced to a man named Mark Goines, a prominent "angel investor" in Silicon Valley start-ups, and, more to the point as things turned out, a member of the Los Altos School Board. Los Altos is a wealthy town with one of the top school systems in California. It is also right next door to my own adopted home, Mountain View—if my house fell into the Los Altos School District, it would immediately be worth $100,000 more because of the schools. Mark and I decided to meet at a local coffee shop one afternoon.

We immediately hit it off. Mark was the type of person who made Silicon Valley what it is. He was super successful, super smart, and, most importantly, unassuming and down-to-earth. We talked a good bit about what the Khan Academy could do and the people it could reach. Half an hour into our conversation, Mark asked what I would do if I could totally reinvent the dynamics of a fifth-grade math class. Assuming this was a purely hypothetical question, I laid out my ideas.

Mark seemed to like what he had heard, but as we stood up after coffee, my assumption was that we'd had a pleasant chat and that was the end of it. Then he said that if I didn't mind, he'd like to discuss my ideas with some other members of the school board.

I should mention in passing that at this juncture things were moving dizzyingly fast for the Khan Academy. It was already clear that Google and the Gates Foundation were going to support us in a big way, and it was making waves in the press. I was getting overwhelmed with meeting requests and the day-to-day of trying to get a real office up and running. I was also getting a bit worried that the whole reason for all of this attention—the videos—was taking a backseat to the nascent operations of the Khan Academy. I clearly needed help, and fast.

I convinced an old friend of mine from Louisiana and then from MIT, Shantanu Sinha, to formally sign on as president and chief operating officer. A brilliant guy who'd been shaming me in academic competitions since we were teenagers, Shantanu gave up a half-million-dollar-a-year, partner track position at McKinsey and Company to come aboard. I found it very reassuring to know that I wasn't the only person crazy enough to give up a relatively safe and remunerative career in exchange for a long-shot chance at helping to rethink education on a global scale.

In early October, Shantanu and I met with Jeff Baier and Alyssa Gallagher, the superintendent and assistant superintendent for Los Altos schools. They listened to our presentation and realized we were proposing the kind of *differentiated education*—that is, teaching geared and nuanced to the needs of each individual student—that educators were always striving for but not quite knowing how to implement. They asked for some time to discuss our ideas with colleagues, principals, and teachers, and then suggested we meet again.

Five days later we got an email from Alyssa saying that they wanted to move forward and start a pilot program in four classrooms after Thanksgiving break—which happened to be a mere five weeks away. So Shantanu and I found ourselves in crunch mode—hiring first-rate designers and engineers, upgrading software, refining ideas. Let me emphasize why we were so passionate about this Los Altos opportunity. Khan Academy had been founded with the goal of reaching students *outside* of any formal setting, and we were already reaching a million students per month even before getting that first funding from Gates and Google. To a large degree, we were successful because we had the luxury of focusing 100 percent on end users rather than having to cater to school districts as some type of software vendor. Based on this, it could have been argued that the Los Altos project was a diversion or even a detour away from our student-focused mission.

But I, and eventually the rest of the team, always dreamt of being more than just a powerful online resource. We felt that we were at a point in history where education could be rethought altogether. We didn't know all the answers—and still don't—but the feeling was that we had to start experimenting in real settings so that we could at least be confident we were asking the right questions. We wanted to learn from real teachers and real students how our technology could be used or be made better. Los Altos was ideal because they were nonbureaucratic, open-minded, and located in the very heart of Silicon Valley. The fact that one of the best school districts in America felt that they could become even more effective by working with us was a huge sign of confidence that we took very seriously.

By the end of November 2010 the pilot program was up and running. Two fifth-grade classes and two seventh-grade classes were being taught math through the Khan Academy. No one, either teachers or students, had been compelled to participate in the program; we worked with the teachers who wanted to work with us. We'd held informational meetings with families and given them the chance to opt out; none did.

There were quite significant differences between the fifth-grade and seventh-grade classes. The fifth graders hadn't been separated into "tracks" yet, and so were probably representative of Los Altos demographics—mainly English-speaking, with college-educated, affluent parents. By seventh grade, however, the students had been tracked, and our program was working with the "developmental" classes, the kids who had fallen behind. Some had learning disabilities; some struggled with English; few had college-educated parents. These students disproportionately came from the "other," much poorer side of El Camino Real (the main avenue in Silicon Valley) that just happened to fall into the Los Altos School District.

But if the two groups had differences, they had similarities as well—mainly enthusiasm and curiosity. Now, as every teacher knows, there are things you can measure and things that you can't. Energy level in a classroom is one of the things you can't plot on a curve but is palpable and important nonetheless. And it was clear from the very start of our program that the energy level had been boosted. Kids were eager to start "Khan time" and some didn't want to go to recess afterwards. They started exploring concepts on their own; they spontaneously began helping one another. In the seventh-grade classes as well as the fifth-grade ones, kids were starting to take control of their learning.

Part of the excitement was that for these students and teachers, the curriculum was developing before their very eyes. But they weren't just watching it develop; they were actively participating in the process—not just accepting change but driving it. Ben Kamens and Jason Rosoff, our software designers who were now doing the heavy lifting on the engineering side, sat in on classes, seeing how kids were actually using and responding to the different features, tweaking this or that according to a teacher's specifications. The feedback loop continually evolved. We started giving kids electronic achievement badges for advancing through concepts—a cost-free way to boost motivation and confidence. Kids came to realize that software was made by real people, and that education was not some monstrous, soulless weight imposed on them, but a living, breathing thing designed for their benefit and *with their help*. Forgive me for gushing, but there was magic going on in those classrooms, and the magic confirmed a belief I'd had ever since talking with my cousins about my earliest video lessons: that the best tools are built when there is open, respectful, two-way conversation between those who make the tools and those who use them.

But okay, it's all well and good to talk about energy and magic and all those feel-good, California-style things; still, I was keenly aware that at the end of the day, the success or failure of the pilot program would be measured not in terms of these intangibles but by the hard-edged, flawed but inevitable, in-your-face criterion of performance on standardized tests. And I admit that as the day grew closer when our students would be taking their respective grade levels of the CSTs (California Standards Tests) I once again got pretty nervous.

But let me be clear about *why* I was nervous. It wasn't that I had strong doubts that our kids were learning math. I was confident they were learning, and that, moreover, they were learning at a deeper and more durable level than most conventional classrooms afforded. My concern, rather, was with the congruence, or lack thereof, between what our kids were learning and what the tests were testing.

This is one of the paradoxes and potential dangers of standardized tests: They measure mastery of a particular curriculum, but not necessarily of the underlying topics and concepts on which the curriculum should be based. The curriculum, in turn, becomes shaped by the expectations of what will be tested. So there's a kind of circular logic, an endless loop going on. Teach what will be tested; test what most likely had been taught. Topics and ideas and levels of understanding that go *beyond* the probable parameters of the test tend to be ignored; they aren't worth the classroom time.

We were trying to enable learning in a different and, we believed, more organic way, a way aimed at conceptual understanding rather than test prep. Because we encouraged students to progress at their own pace, we had some very advanced fifth graders already working on algebra and even trigonometry. But this impressive advancement would go unrecognized on the CSTs, which only tested proficiency in the usual fifth-grade material. Further, with regard to the fifth-grade classes, we were up against some pretty tough comparisons, as 91 percent of students in conventional Los Altos classes were already testing as "proficient" or "advanced" for their grade level.

With regard to the seventh-grade classes, we had a somewhat different set of concerns. These students had been significantly underperforming their peers before participating in the pilot program; they badly needed remediation. Would our unconventional approach have provided it?

Test day came. We crossed our fingers and waited for results. When they came in, they were overwhelmingly positive.

Our fifth graders posted a stellar 96 percent at proficient or advanced grade level. I do have to say that a good bit of this outperformance was probably due to the amazing teachers in the pilot classes rather than just our resources. It did decisively prove to the district that despite the fact that our software was still at a nascent state and that we weren't teaching to the test, the experiment was definitely not doing any harm. In light of the test results, coupled with the positive feedback from teachers, students, and parents, the board decided to use the Khan Academy as part of the math curriculum for all fifth- and sixth-grade math classes in the district for the following school year. In keeping with the Pinball Philosophy, we had done well at the game and so were being allowed to play again.

But the truly dramatic results were with the seventh-grade

classes. Relative to a year prior, their average score on the grade level exam improved by 106 percent. Twice as many students were now at grade level. A handful of students jumped two categories, from "below basic" to "proficient." A few even leap-frogged into the "advanced" category. As gratifying as these results were to us, it was equally pleasing to tap one more nail into the coffin of tracking. Our underserved, underperforming, and purportedly "slow" kids were now operating at the same—or higher—level as their more affluent peers.

I want to emphasize this last point. Remedial math classes are often viewed as something of an academic graveyard. Once students are deemed "slow," they tend to fall farther and farther behind their peers. Now, all of a sudden, we were seeing that students who were put in the "slower" math classes could actually leapfrog *ahead* of their "non-slow" peers. Even better, the experience with both the fifth and seventh graders showed that there really was no reason to track students into separate classrooms to begin with. Now every student could work at his or her own pace; it was unpredictable who could eventually advance the most. It should be noted that this initial data came from a very small data set, a handful of classrooms, and was not designed as a truly controlled experiment. It did, however, point in a very promising direction.

By the summer of 2011, we began ramping up our team to manage a district-wide pilot with twelve hundred students in Los Altos. Many, many more teachers and schools were also eager to work with us. Given that we wanted to push our own learning and see how the Khan Academy could be applied in different use cases, we chose a handful of public, charter, and private schools in California that served very different types of students—seventy classrooms in total. Because all of the student and teacher tools we were using with our pilots were available for anyone to use, it became clear from our server data that there were also more than ten thousand teacher-led classrooms or cohorts, serving 350,000 students around the world, that were using us independently of any formal pilot program.

At the time of this writing, we are just beginning to get data from this larger wave of pilots, but the preliminary information seems even more exciting than what we saw from the first, limited pilot in Los Altos.

Let's consider the Oakland Unity High School pilot, where 95 percent of the students are African American or Latino and 85 percent receive free or reduced lunch. First the subjective. In a recent blog post, David Castillo, the principal, and Peter McIntosh, a math teacher, wrote about how in previous years they "found that students failed to engage in the coursework and spent little to no time studying." They went on to describe how "students were disengaged from their learning responsibilities and the derailing of their studying began as early as elementary school." However, their descriptions of what is culturally happening in their pilot classrooms is exciting. They wrote:

> We believe that our use of Khan Academy is resulting in a fundamental change in student character—with responsibility replacing apathy and effort replacing laziness. We believe that this character change is the primary reason behind the stunning results we are beginning

to experience—at both the class level and in individual students.

And the data from the students' tests scores is indeed exciting. Students are scoring 10 to 40 percent higher on average across a battery of exams covering different domains in algebra. The percentage of students showing reasonable proficiency in various topic areas is even more significant. For example, the percentage of students who now scored at least 80 percent on their recently administered "Systems of Equations" exam grew by a factor of four. It is perhaps too early to pick out a trend, but it looks like the relative improvement compared to prior years is only growing more dramatic as the class moves into more and more advanced topics.

We're getting similar results from the other pilots. A group of sixth graders had entered the KIPP pilot from local Oakland public schools with a roughly third-grade-level mastery of math. Six months later, most of the class was operating at fifth- and sixth-grade levels. The teachers had never seen groups of students move ahead two and three grade levels in a matter of months. We are hoping to see much, much more data like this in the months to come.

Education for All Ages

Anyone who stops learning is old, whether at twenty or eighty. Anyone who keeps learning stays young. The greatest thing in life is to keep your mind young.

—HENRY FORD

It is utterly false and cruelly arbitrary to put all the play and learning into childhood, all the work into middle age, and all the regrets into old age.

—MARGARET MEAD

Please bear with me now as I segue into a very different sort of intersection between the Khan Academy and the real world— the real world of grown-ups interested in lifelong learning and in maintaining active minds.

Back in 2008, when the worldwide credit crisis was paralyzing markets and causing banks to fail, I, like everybody else, was trying to figure out just what the heck was going on. The issues were quite complicated, the technical jargon was fairly daunting, and I think it's fair to say that some on Wall Street and in the government preferred to keep the rest of us a bit confused. So I tried to break through to a reasonable level of understanding in the way that comes most naturally to me—by breaking the subject down into manageable but clearly inter-connected chunks and making sure I had a conceptual grasp of one aspect of the problem before moving on to the next. Because it was clear to me that many other people were also grappling with these suddenly pressing economic riddles— What, exactly, was a collateralized debt obligation? How did the Treasury Department relate to the Federal Reserve? What is quantitative easing and how is it different than just print-ing money?—I started posting video lessons about the banking crisis. To be honest, I didn't give a lot of thought to the ques-tion of who exactly the videos were *for*. I did them because I felt the need to do them.

Then a completely unexpected thing happened. Almost as soon as the videos went live, I started hearing from profes-sional journalists and commentators who'd watched them— business writers, financial advisers, anchors of TV shows about economics and investing. (I even got a somewhat scary email from an investment banker thanking me for my video explain-ing mortgage-backed securities. The gist of the message was, *Thanks, now I understand what I do for a living.*) At the peak of the crisis, CNN invited me to speak on their network, to do a sort of live fifteen-minute lesson complete with my electronic blackboard.

This experience and the feedback I received from it convinced me that Khan Academy had a duty to do much more than just present standard academic topics for traditional school-age students. There was a deep need to help educate people of all ages regarding the ever-changing dynamics of the world around them. With the world becoming more and more complex, true democracy—not to mention peace of mind—was at risk if average folks couldn't understand what was happening and why.

This realization, in turn, led to an even more basic question about the artificial boundaries of formal education. Why does "education" stop at some point? Why isn't it lifelong? Doesn't it seem arbitrary and in fact a little tragic that we invest so much in learning through formal education for twelve or sixteen or twenty years, and then just turn off the spigot when we reach full adulthood?

Some studies suggest that most people stop learning new things in their thirties. I use the word "suggest" advisedly, since studies on such a vast and amorphous subject can never be precise or absolute. *Some* people keep learning. Almost everyone learns *something* every day. As sentient human beings, how could we not? Still, the basic point is tough to deny. At some point in life, learning new things becomes less of a priority. At some fulcrum moment, we have learned most of what we will ever know. The learning curve flattens out. Except for the laziest or most incurious among us, it doesn't flatline altogether. We get blips here and there from travel, from hobbies, from a new everyday technology that forces us to stretch our awareness of how things work. But for the most part we confront life equipped with things we've learned before—sometimes *long* before. New knowledge becomes a smaller and smaller part of the mix. The problem is that as the pace of change accelerates all around us, the ability to learn new things may be the most important skill of all. Is it realistic to expect adults to be able to do this?

The answer is a resounding yes. According to a recent paper issued by the Royal Society of London, "the brain has extraordinary adaptability, sometimes referred to as 'neuroplasticity.' This is due to the process by which connections between neurons are strengthened when they are simultaneously activated; often summarized as, 'neurons that fire together wire together.' The effect is known as experience-dependent plasticity *and is present throughout life*" (italics added).[2]

Not only is the ability to learn lifelong, but, within certain limits, it is in our power to maximize and guide this ability. As we saw earlier in our brief discussion of neuroscience and memory, handling and storing information in the brain is a physical process. It takes energy; it burns calories; it leads to the synthesis of new proteins and the alteration of existing ones. In all these regards, brainwork is closely analogous to physical exercise, and likewise subject to the rule of use-it-or-lose-it. Moreover, we don't simply choose to exercise our brains or not; we can even choose which *parts* of our brains to work on. One fascinating aspect of the Royal Society's report concerned a study of London cabdrivers. Faced with the necessity of learning every nook and cranny of London's famously difficult geography, the cabbies literally grew "extra" gray matter in the parts of their brains dedicated to spatial relations and navigation. When the drivers retired and no longer exercised their navigational skills, their brain volume in those areas diminished. Similar studies have been done on musicians and even jugglers, with consistent findings; when knowledge or skill is acquired or enhanced, there is ongoing neural development in the part of the brain where that specific subject or skill is based.

It must be said that not all the news from neuroscience is good when it comes to the capacity for lifelong learning. Certain aspects of neural plasticity do diminish with age. The older brain has a tougher time assembling the most basic building blocks of learning. This makes it somewhat more challenging for adults to learn entirely new things and explains, for example, why it seems to be easier to learn a foreign language early in life. On the other hand, adults seem to be better at learning *by association*. With a bigger knowledge base to begin with, and long-established habits of logic and deduction, grown-ups are more likely to grasp new concepts by way of their connections to ideas already known.[3]

This suggests that, all things considered, learning is not necessarily easier or harder at one stage of life or another, but that our approach to learning might be different in adulthood. There's even a separate word to describe this approach and the teaching methods most appropriate to it: *androgogy*. This is in contrast to the more familiar *pedagogy*, broadly defined as the art and science of teaching children. The key difference? Pedagogy puts the emphasis on the teacher; the teacher decides what will be learned, when it will be learned, and how the learning will be tested. Androgogy, on the other hand, puts the emphasis and the responsibility on the learner himself. Adults don't have to learn; they *choose* to learn. This active choosing and the motivation behind it serve to focus our attention and thereby make learning easier. As it was expressed by Malcolm Knowles in his seminal book *The Adult Learner*, "If we know *why* we are learning and if the reason fits our needs as we perceive them, we will learn quickly and deeply."[4]

All of the above seems to indicate that the Khan Academy approach dovetails very neatly with the needs and inclinations of adult learners. Adult learners are, above all, self-motivated; Internet-based video lessons that are available at the learner's convenience certainly tap into this self-motivation. Likewise, that the lessons are self-paced pays due respect to adults' sense of responsibility and self-knowledge; learners take in as much or as little as they can handle in a sitting; they can attend to their learning as their complicated schedules allow. Moreover, as we have seen, adults seem to learn most easily and naturally by associating new knowledge and concepts with things already known, and it is absolutely basic to Khan Academy principles to emphasize these connections—to teach in accordance with the way the grown-up mind works anyway.

There is a certain irony here. I entered teaching as the tutor of a twelve-year-old girl. To be perfectly honest, adult education was an afterthought. In fact, I'll go further. As I muddled along in my tinkering and pragmatic way, without assumptions or theory, I really didn't consider lifelong learning at all. Yet it turns out that what I was trying to accomplish with the kids was to foster an atmosphere and an attitude that came closer to that of adult learners. I inadvertently bumped into an idea that Knowles had already explored: Maybe androgogy—self-directed learning with the teacher as guide rather than director—may be more appropriate for *everyone*.

PART 4

The One World Schoolhouse

Embracing Uncertainty

Here is a remarkable thought: Among the world's children starting grade school this year, 65 percent will end up doing jobs that haven't even been invented yet.

This projection, while impossible to prove, comes from a highly respected and responsible source, Cathy N. Davidson, a Duke University professor who is also the codirector of the MacArthur Foundation Digital Media and Learning Competitions.[1] And after all, once we get over the shock of that sheer number, the projection seems entirely plausible. Grade school students in the 1960s had no way of foreseeing that the hot spot in job creation and economic growth during the 1970s and '80s would come from various aspects of the personal computing industry—an industry that didn't exist in the Age of Woodstock. As recently as the 1980s, no one planned to make his or her living through the Internet, since the Internet existed nowhere but in the hushed and secret corridors of DARPA. Even more recently, how many kids, teachers, or parents realized that little Sally might end up working in advanced genomics, while Johnny became an entrepreneur in social media, Tabitha became an engineer in cloud computing, and Pedro designed apps for iPhones?

None of these developments was foreseeable ten or fifteen years before the fact, and given the tendency of change to feed on itself and keep accelerating, it's a safe bet that a decade from today there will be even more surprises. No one is smart enough to know what will happen tomorrow—or, for that matter, in the next hour, minute, or nanosecond—let alone half a generation down the line.

The certainty of change, coupled with the complete *un*certainty as to the precise nature of the change, has profound and complex implications for our approach to education. For me, though, the most basic takeaway is crystal clear: Since we can't predict exactly what today's young people will need to know in ten or twenty years, *what* we teach them is less important than *how* they learn to teach themselves.

Sure, kids need to have a grounding in basic math and science; they need to understand how language works so they can communicate effectively and with nuance; they should have some awareness of history and politics so as to feel at home in the world, and some conversance with art in order to appreciate the human thirst for the sublime. Beyond these fundamentals, however, the crucial task of education is to teach kids *how* to learn. To lead them to *want* to learn. To nurture curiosity, to encourage wonder, and to instill confidence so that later on they'll have the tools for finding answers to the many questions we don't yet know how to ask.

In these regards, conventional education, with its emphasis on rote memorization, artificially sequestered concepts, and one-size-fits-all curricula geared too narrowly toward testing, is clearly failing us. At a time when unprecedented change demands unprecedented flexibility, conventional education continues to be brittle. As our increasingly interconnected world cries out for more minds, more innovators, more of a spirit of inclusion, conventional education continues to discourage and exclude. At a time of stubborn and worldwide economic difficulties, the conventional educational establishment seems oddly blind (or tragically resistant) to readily available technology-based solutions for making education not only better but more affordable, accessible to far more people in far more places.

In the pages that follow, I would like to propose a different sort of future for education—a more inclusive and more creative future. My vision may strike some people as a peculiar mix of ideas, because some of what I'm suggesting is quite new and some of it is very old; some of it is based on technology that has only recently come into being, and some of it harkens back to bygone wisdom about how kids actually learn and grow. Yes, I am a firm believer in the transformative power of computers and the Internet. Paradoxically, though, I am urging us forward, in part, by suggesting a return to certain older models and methods that have been cast aside in the name of "progress."

My Background as a Student

When I was in tenth grade, I had an experience that proved pivotal not only for my own schooling but for the development of my entire philosophy of education. At a regional math competition in Louisiana, I first met Shantanu Sinha—the same Shantanu who is now president of the Academy. He was an acknowledged math jock, and he quickly showed me my place in the world when he beat me in the finals of the competition. But there was something else about Shantanu that impressed me even more than his sheer prowess. Chatting during the contest, he told me that as a tenth grader he was already studying pre-calculus. I myself was still taking Algebra II, although the subject had ceased to be stimulating. My understanding was that I *had* to stay in Algebra II, because that's what tenth graders were taught, and there was nothing to discuss. Shantanu told me that he'd *tested out* of algebra and had therefore been allowed to advance.

Testing out. What a concept. I'd had no idea that such a thing existed, though even a moment's thought suggested that it made perfect sense. If a student could demonstrate proficiency with a certain set of ideas and processes, why not let him or her move on to more advanced ones?

Back at my own school, full of enthusiasm, full of hope, I approached the powers that be with the possibility of testing out of my math class. My suggestion was instantly shot down by way of a dreary and all too familiar argument: *If we let you do it, we'd have to let everybody do it.*

Since I was as self-involved as most people at that age, I had no interest in what other kids did or didn't get to do; I only cared that I myself had been denied, so I sulked and misbehaved (although I did have the therapeutic release of being the lead singer in a heavy metal band). Over time, however, a broader and rather subversive question started scratching at my mind; eventually it became one of my most basic educational beliefs: If kids can advance at their own pace, and if they'd be happier and more productive that way, why *not* let everybody do it?

Where was the harm? Wouldn't kids learn more, wouldn't their curiosity and imagination be better nourished, if they were allowed to follow their instincts and take on new challenges as they were able? If the student graduated early, wouldn't this free up scarce resources for the students who needed it? True, this approach would call for more flexibility and more close attention to students *as individual learners.* To be sure, there were technical and logistical hurdles to be cleared; there were long and brittle habits that would need to be altered. But whom was education supposed to serve, after all? Was the main idea to keep school boards and vice principals in their comfort zone, or was the main idea to help students grow as thinking people?

Looking back, I think that in some odd and embryonic way, it was that stupid and infuriating statement—*If we let you do it, we'd have to let everybody do it*—that cemented my commitment to self-paced learning and started me on the path of trying to make self-paced learning a possibility for everyone.

Eventually I was able to take the math classes I wanted—but only by working around and in some sense defying the system that was in place. I started taking summer courses at a local college. My high school then "allowed" me to take basic calculus, the only calculus course they offered. I got hold of a more advanced textbook and studied on my own. My senior year I spent more time at the University of New Orleans than at my own high school.

I was fortunate to come from a family and a community that placed a very high priority on education; my mother supported and abetted my efforts to work around the system. But what about the kids whose parents didn't care as much or were afraid to rock the boat or simply didn't know how to help? What became of their potential, of the intellectual curiosity that had been systematically drained out of them?

If high school persuaded me of the crucial importance of independent study and self-paced learning, it took college to convince me of the incredible inefficiency, irrelevance, and even inhumanity of the standard broadcast lecture.

When I first arrived at MIT, I was frankly intimidated by the brainpower around me. Among my freshman cohort were kids who had represented the United States or Russia in the Math Olympiad. My very first physics lab was taught by a professor who'd won a Nobel Prize for experimentally verifying the existence of the quark. Everyone seemed smarter than I was, and aside from that it was *cold*! I'd never seen snow before or felt anything quite as chilly as the wind off the Charles River. Fortunately, there were a few other Louisiana kids around; one of them was Shantanu, who now went from being a high school acquaintance to a good friend and college roommate.

As we settled into the MIT routine, Shantanu and I began independently to arrive at the same subversive but increasingly obvious conclusion: The giant lecture classes were a monumental waste of time. Three hundred students crammed into a stifling lecture hall; one professor droning through a talk he knew by heart and had delivered a hundred times before. The sixty-minute talks were bad enough; the ninety-minute talks were torture. What was the point? Was this education or an endurance contest? Was anybody actually learning anything? Why did students show up at all? Shantanu and I came up with two basic theories about this. Kids went to the lectures either because their parents were paying *x* number of dollars per, or because many of the lecturers were academic celebrities, so there was an element of show business involved.

Be that as it may, we couldn't help noticing that many of the students who religiously attended every lecture were the same ones most desperately cramming the night before the exam. Why? The reason, it seemed to me, was that until the cramming phase they'd approached the subject matter only *passively*. They'd dutifully sat in class and let concepts wash over them; they'd expected to learn by osmosis, but it hadn't quite worked out because they'd never really *engaged*. To be clear, I don't blame my fellow students for finding themselves in this situation; as good and diligent pupils, they'd put their faith in what was, after all, the prescribed approach. Unfortunately, as we've seen in our discussion of attention spans and active versus passive learning, the prescribed approach was completely out of synch with the realities of human capability.

Shantanu and I soon found ourselves a part of a small but visible and slightly notorious MIT subculture—the class skippers. I don't recommend this for everyone, but it worked for us. To be sure, skipping class can easily become an excuse for, or a symptom of, simply goofing off. To us, honestly, it seemed like a more productive and responsible use of our time. Would we learn more sitting passively in a lecture for an hour and a half, or engaging *actively* with a textbook—or with online videos and interactive assessments, if only they'd been available at the time? Would we be more enriched by watching a professor's presentation, or by deriving equations and writing software ourselves? Even as freshmen, we concluded that our class-skipping approach was working; we didn't need to cram at the end of a semester and we didn't stress about solving problems on a test, because that's what we'd been doing all along.

We soon became acquainted with some upperclassmen who were taking eight or nine courses a term (about double the typical MIT student's already rigorous course load), and who challenged us to take extra courses as well. Without doubt, these guys were bright, but not freakishly so; their argument, in fact, was that *any* of us—not just at MIT but at every high school and university—should be able to handle twice as many courses *if we avoided the seat time and simply pursued whatever actually helped us learn.* There was no hocus-pocus here, no miracle shortcuts to academic success. It took discipline and work, quite a lot of each. But the idea was to work *effectively*, naturally, and independently.

I want to pause a moment to consider this somewhat radical thought, which dovetailed perfectly with my own beliefs and in turn helped shape my eventual approach to teaching and learning. Could people actually learn twice as much as was generally expected of them? It seemed ambitious...but why not? As we saw in the discussion of the Prussian roots of our school system, the original aim of educators was not necessarily to produce the smartest students possible, but to turn out tractable and standardized citizens, workers who knew *enough*. To this end, attention was given not to what students *could* learn, but to the bare minimum of what they had to learn.

Now, I am not imputing such Machiavellian motives to contemporary educators; but I am suggesting that some of the habits and assumptions that have come down from the eighteenth-century model still steer and limit what students learn. Conventional curricula don't only tell students where to start; they tell students where to stop. A series of lessons ends; that subject is *over*. Why aren't students encouraged to go farther and deeper—to learn *twice* as much? Probably for the same reason we consider 70 percent a passing grade. Our standards are too low. We're so squeamish and embarrassed about the very notion of "failure" that we end up diluting and devaluing the idea of success. We limit what students believe they can do by selling short what we expect them to do.

Coming back to MIT, Shantanu and I did take on something close to double course loads, and we both graduated with high GPAs and multiple degrees. And it wasn't because we were any smarter or harder-working than our peers. It was because we didn't waste time sitting passively in class. Understand, this is not a knock against MIT itself, which I thought was a magical place full of dazzlingly creative people doing amazing things. Further, MIT was very forward-thinking in letting students take as many courses as they wanted. My criticism is not of the institution but of the tired old habit of the passive lecture.

Replace that with active learning, and I believe that most and very possibly all of us are capable of taking in much more than is currently expected of us. We can go much farther, and get there far more efficiently, with self-paced study, mentoring, and hands-on experiences. We can reach more ambitious goals if we are given the latitude to set those goals for ourselves.

The Spirit of the One Room Schoolhouse

Most educated people today attended school with children their own age and then remained with this same age-determined cohort throughout their elementary and secondary education, and even onward through college and graduate school. This basic model—grouping kids by birth date and then advancing them together grade by grade—is such a fundamental aspect of conventional education that people seldom seem to think about it. But we should, because its implications are huge.

First of all, let's remember that this age-group pattern did not always exist; like everything else about our educational habits, it is a human construct and a response to certain conditions in certain places and times. Before the Industrial Revolution, it was very much the exception to lump schoolkids together by age; it just wasn't practical, given that most people lived on farms and the population was spread very thin. With industrialization came urbanization, and the new population density set the stage for multiroom schools. Kids needed to be divided up somehow, and forming classes by age seemed a logical choice. But there was a whole raft of implications that went along with sequestering kids by age, and these have turned out to be a very mixed blessing.

Not to pick on the Prussians again, but as we've seen, the Prussian model is largely based on dividing human knowledge into artificially constrained chunks. Massive and flowing areas of human thought are diced up into stand-alone "subjects." The school day is rigorously divided into "periods," such that when the bell rings, discussion and exploration are lopped off. The strict grouping of students by age provides yet another axis along which education could be sliced up, compartmentalized, and therefore controlled.

Arguably, this separation by age is the most powerful division of all, because it has allowed for the development of set curricula and ultimately arbitrary but consensual standards of what kids should learn at a given grade level. Expectations move in lockstep, as though all eight- or ten- or twelve-year-olds were interchangeable. Once kids were grouped by age, targets seemed clear and testing was straightforward. It all seemed quite scientific and advanced, and it proved very convenient for administrators. But little or no attention was paid to what was lost along the way.

To state what should be obvious, there is nothing natural about segregating kids by age. That isn't how families work; it isn't what the world looks like; and it runs counter to the way that kids have learned and socialized for most of human history. Even the Mickey Mouse Club included kids of different ages, and as anyone who's ever spent time around children can tell you, both younger and older kids benefit when different ages mix. The older ones take responsibility for the younger ones. (I see this even between my three-year-old and my one-year-old—and, trust me, it's a remarkable thing to behold.) The younger ones look up to and emulate the older ones. Everyone seems to act more mature. Both younger and older rise to the occasion.

Take away this mix of ages and everybody loses something. Younger kids lose heroes and idols and mentors. Perhaps even more damagingly, older kids are deprived of a chance to be leaders, to exercise responsibility, and are thereby infantilized.

Let's consider this a moment. Of late there has been much hand-wringing about the state of mind of contemporary teenagers—a seemingly widespread malaise found everywhere from New York to Berlin to Bahrain, and whose symptoms run the gamut from mere slackerism all the way to suicide. I would suggest that at least a significant part of the problem is our failure to entrust adolescents with real responsibility. Yes, we stress them out with demands and competition... but only to do with *themselves*. We deny them the chance to mentor or help others, and we thereby conspire in their isolation and self-involvement. Biologically, kids start becoming grown-ups around the age of twelve. That's when they can reproduce, and while I'm certainly not advocating teenage parenthood, I do believe that nature would not have made it possible unless adolescents were also wired to be ready to take responsibility for others. High school kids are burgeoning adults, but by narrowly restricting them to the companionship of their peers, responsible for no one but themselves, we treat them as children—and children they tend to remain.

For the above reasons, I believe that the school of the future should be built around an updated version of the one-room schoolhouse. Kids of different ages should mix. Without the tyranny of the broadcast lecture and the one-size-fits-all curriculum, there is no reason this can't be done. With self-paced learning established as the basic model, there's no reason to lump kids by age, still less to "track" them based on perceived potential. The older or more advanced students become allies of the teacher by mentoring and tutoring the kids who are behind. Younger students benefit by having a range of role models, big brothers and big sisters. Older kids sharpen and refine their understanding of concepts in the act of explaining them to younger kids. No one is just a student; everyone is a teacher as well, worthy of the respect that goes with that. And the schoolroom, rather than being an artificial cloister shut off from the rest of life, comes to more closely resemble the world beyond its walls—and therefore to better prepare students to function and to flourish in that world.

This idea of the age-mixed classroom is not some unrealistic fantasy. It is already being experimented with in one of the best schools in the country—Marlborough School, an all-girls prep school in Los Angeles. Last year, I was introduced to one of their students, India Yaffe, who had won an essay-writing competition called the Guerin Prize, in which the students write about someone they would like to meet. In what I can only consider bad judgment on the part of a teenager, she wanted to meet me.

So India, her dad, and the head of the school's math department, Dr. Chris Talone, came to visit. Beyond just chatting about education and math in general, Dr. Talone expressed interest in working with the Khan Academy in some way. I said I'd be game if they were willing to push the envelope—namely, use Khan Academy to facilitate a math class that didn't separate students by age. They agreed that it was an approach worth trying. So we designed an inclusive class, using Khan Academy video lessons and feedback software, to be taught by Dr. Talone for students representing every level of math from pre-algebra to AP calculus. The ground rules stipulated that the course material be at least as rigorous as the instruction in the regular and honors-level math classes at Marlborough, and that students at every grade level would in fact come away fully prepared for their next level in the math sequence.

At the time of this writing, the class is in its sixth month and all the evidence we've seen and heard suggests that it is magical. Seventh graders are working alongside girls all the way up to twelfth grade. They are all working on what they need to work on. They have access to their peers and an amazing teacher when they need it. The girls are learning more and are less stressed. I've been told that the biggest problem has been resentment from girls who weren't able to get in on the experiment.

Teaching as a Team Sport

Conventional classroom teaching is one of the loneliest jobs in the world. Surrounded by a sea of kids, the teacher is like a lone rock in a bay. Sure, there's the faculty lounge where one can have a cup of coffee, a brief chat, maybe even sneak a cigarette...but when a teacher is actually doing his work, he's out there all alone. There's no peer support, no one to consult with, no one to ask for help or confirmation. There's no buddy in the next cubicle with whom to shed some tension, no extra set of eyes to deal with the dizzying peripheral business of a real live classroom.

This should change so that teachers can have some of the practical and emotional benefits that pertain in nearly every other profession—the chance to help each other, lean on each other when necessary, to mentor and be mentored by colleagues.

As a corollary of having mixed-age classes, I would also propose maintaining student/teacher ratios, but merging classrooms together. Now that students can all learn at their own pace, we no longer need the artificial separation of classrooms that are designed for students to listen to a lecture from one teacher. To be clear, I'm not suggesting either a net loss or a net gain of teaching positions. But rather than three or four separate classes of twenty-five kids and one lonesome teacher, I would suggest a class of seventy-five to a hundred students with *three or four* teachers. To me there are several clear advantages to this, all of which stem from the enhancement of *flexibility* in a system such as this.

In a one-teacher classroom, what you get is...one teacher. There are only so many techniques that a single teacher can deploy. In a class with multiple teachers, the permutations expand exponentially (actually factorially, but you get the picture). Where appropriate, teachers can teach in tandem— taking different sides, say, in a debate, or working with different small teams on project-building. In other instances, a particular teacher might have special expertise on a topic, and would handle that piece on her own. Or again, since everyone needs downtime, team teachers could easily rotate in and out, thereby avoiding the disruption and inefficiency that usually accompanies the appearance of the dreaded "substitute."

Most basically, since teaching is a complex and multifaceted job, and since no two people have the exact same set of strengths and weaknesses, a multiple-teacher arrangement would give each teacher the chance to focus on what he or she does best. Further, since there's no such thing as a single *right* way to teach or a single *right* way to approach a subject, students would have the benefit of being exposed to a number of different, nuanced perspectives; this would help them to become critical thinkers, and provide better preparation for dealing with a world of widely divergent viewpoints and opinions.

In emotional as well as pedagogic ways, a multiteacher classroom makes sense. Given the mysteries of human personality, certain kids and certain teachers will always discover affinities that become the basis for important bonds; having several teachers in a classroom allows more opportunities for this magic to occur.

Finally, I believe a multiple-teacher system would go a long way toward solving the very serious problem of teacher burnout. Giving teachers more professional companionship and real-time peer support would make their work less stressful. As in almost every other field, teachers would now be able to observe and mentor each other. Younger teachers would learn from more experienced ones. Older teachers would absorb energy and fresh ideas from newer ones. Everyone would benefit from being less isolated.

Speaking of teamwork, have you ever noticed that some kids tend to loathe and detest their teachers but worship and adore their coaches?

On the face of it, this is absurd. Both teachers and coaches are there to help. Both ask students to push themselves to do difficult things—not infrequently, things that kids claim they really hate to do, such as deriving equations or running wind sprints. Yet students' stance vis-à-vis their teachers is often adversarial, while their attitude toward coaches tends to be enthusiastic and cooperative. Why the dramatic difference?

Part of it, of course, is simply that teachers represent what students *have* to do, while coaches represent what they've chosen to do. But I would argue that this alone does not explain the dichotomy. I believe that a big part of the reason kids revere and obey their coaches is that the coaches are specifically and explicitly *on the student's side*. Coaches are helping them be the best they can be, so that they can experience the thrill of winning. In team sports, coaches inculcate the atavistic spirit and focus of a hunting clan. In individual sports, the coach stands tall as the main if not the only ally. When kids win, coaches celebrate along with them; when they lose, the coach is there to comfort and to find a lesson in defeat.

By contrast, from the perspective of many students, teachers are not viewed as someone who is on their side. They are not viewed as someone preparing them for competition with an adversary. Unfortunately, they are often seen as the adversary themselves—someone who throws busywork and disjointed formulas at them in order to make sure they have no free time and humiliate them. Is this viewpoint fair? Of course not. Most teachers care at least as much about their students as a coach does. So why does it happen?

It happens because teachers are forced to drag students along at a set pace in a system where assessments are used to label people rather than to help them master concepts that will be relevant in succeeding in a very competitive world. Let's face it—teachers no less than coaches are preparing kids for a world of competition, but that message is seldom made explicit.

In fact, the only way to do it would be to make clear that what happens in the classroom is but preparation for real competition in the outside world. That the exams aren't there to label and humiliate you; they are there to fine-tune your abilities. That when you have identified deficiencies, it doesn't mean that you are dumb; it means that you have something to work on. The teacher will make it their priority to make sure you repair those weak points and not artificially push you to the next topic on which you will have even more difficulty. The teacher, like a coach, needs to emphasize that anything less than mastery won't do because he or she expects you to be the best thinker and creator that you can be.

Ordered Chaos Is a
Good Thing

Picture the stereotype of a perfectly run conventional class-room. Desks are arranged in tidy ranks and rows as on a chess-board. Students deploy their notebooks at parallel slants, their pencils poised in unison, like the bows of a violin section. All eyes are on the teacher looming at the front of the room. Silence reigns but for the first tap of her chalk against the blackboard. It's a decorous and fitting atmosphere...for a funeral.

The ideal classroom, in my opinion, would look and sound quite different.

As I've said, I would group together as many as a hundred students of widely varying ages. They would seldom if ever all be doing the same thing at the same time. And while nooks and alcoves within this imagined school might be perfectly quiet for private study, other parts would be bustling with col-laborative chatter.

At a given moment, perhaps one-fifth of the students would be doing computer-based lessons and exercises aimed at a deep and durable grasp of core concepts. Let me pause a moment to stress this: *one-fifth of the students*. This is another way of saying that only one-fifth of the school day, or one to two hours, would be spent on the Khan Academy lessons (or some future version thereof) and any peer tutoring that it might catalyze. Given the greatly increased efficiency of self-paced, mastery-based learning, one or two hours is enough, and this should ease the concerns of any technophobes out there who fear that technology-based education means that kids would sit numbly in front of computer screens all day. That's neither true nor necessary. An hour or two suffices—and, as we've already discussed, even that time involves significant peer-to-peer tutoring and one-on-one time with teachers.

But let's come back to the rest of the students. Twenty kids out of a hundred are working at computers, with one of our team teachers circulating among them, answering questions, troubleshooting difficulties *as they occur*. The feedback and the help are virtually immediate, and the twenty-to-one ratio is augmented by peer-to-peer tutoring and mentoring—a central advantage of the age-mixed classroom.

What of the other eighty students?

I can see (and hear!) a boisterous subgroup learning economics and trying out market simulations by way of board games such as those we've used with good effect at our summer camps.

I would have another group, divided into teams, building robots or designing mobile apps or testing out novel ways for structures to capture sunlight.

A quiet corner or room could be devoted to students working on art or creative writing projects. A less quiet corner would be reserved for those working on original music. Clearly, it would be an advantage to have a team teacher with particular affinities for those fields.

The most important aspect of this is that it would carve out space and time for open-ended thinking and creativity for all students. In today's schools, it's not hard to find "different-thinking" students who are too often neglected, misunderstood, and either alienated or simply left behind by rigid standard curricula. I'm talking about the kind of kid who might prove to be brilliant but at certain snapshot moments is regarded as slow, or the kind of kid whose interests zig off in peculiar directions that the rest of the class simply doesn't have time or interest to follow. The kid who becomes obsessed with solid geometry and isn't ready to let it go when the lesson ends, but rather wants to derive its equations and spin out its implications all on his own. Or the kid who is happiest racking her brain over a math problem that might not even have a solution. Or formulating an approach in engineering that has never even been tried.

These are the kinds of curious, mysterious, and original minds that often end up making major contributions to our world; to reach their full potential, however, they need the latitude to follow their own oblique, nonstandard paths. That latitude is seldom found in a conventional, box-shaped classroom in which everyone is supposed to be doing the exact same lesson, and "differentness" is generally used as a negative. To a large degree, these students just haven't allowed themselves to be molded to the Prussian ideal. And I believe many, many more students can be like them if we allow them to. I believe a school in which they could cover basic course material in one or two hours a day, leaving plenty of time—not interrupted by bells every hour—and space for their private mulling in a supportive environment, would allow most kids to thrive academically, creatively, and emotionally. The actual physical layout of the room could be experimented with; in theory this could even occur in existing classrooms or an open field. The important difference between what I am describing and today's classrooms is that any walls would be only superficial physical boundaries, not mental ones.

Redefining Summer

I realize that this next suggestion won't win me any popularity contests, but I stand by it anyway: If we are to bring education into the twentieth century—still less the twenty-first!—we need to radically rethink the whole idea of summer vacation.

Of all the outmoded ideas and customs that have made contemporary education inefficient and inappropriate to our needs, summer vacation is among the most egregious. It's a carryover from a world that no longer exists, an agrarian relic on a citified globe. It made sense in, say, 1730, when most people lived on farms. Families needed to eat before they could worry about their children getting educated; kids of all ages and both genders were expected to help in the fields. That was then. Has anyone in the education establishment noticed that, at least in the industrialized nations, the world hasn't really looked that way for the last century or two?

As currently conceived, summer vacation is a monumental waste of time and money. Around the world, tens or hundreds of billions of dollars in education infrastructure—school buildings, labs, gymnasiums—sits vacant or at the very least seriously underutilized. Teachers don't teach and administrators don't administer. Worst of all, of course, is that students don't learn. It would be bad enough if summer vacation constituted simply a pause in learning; even that would be a negative, as continuity would be broken and momentum would be lost. As everyone knows, it's easier to keep pedaling a bicycle than to start one again after a stop; why should the process be any different with learning?

In point of fact, however, the most serious downside of summer vacation isn't just that kids stop learning; it's that they almost immediately start unlearning. As we saw in our brief discussion of neuroscience, what we call "learning" has a physical correlative in the synthesis of new proteins and the construction of new neural pathways in the brain. Those pathways are strengthened by repetition and also by association. They are weakened by disuse, and if the disuse continues, the circuits eventually break down; what we call "unlearning" is the atrophy of neural pathways we used to have. Give a kid ten weeks off from school, and it's neither metaphor nor exaggeration to say that some of what he used to know about algebra has vanished from his brain and been reabsorbed into his bloodstream, where it does him no good at all for solving quadratic equations or mastering later concepts.

Before being branded a complete antivacation ogre, let me make clear that I am not blind to the beauty of summer or the value of time away from the school routine. There are many kinds of learning and enrichment that can flourish when school is not in session. Wealthy families have the luxury of traveling with their children, broadening their horizons and showing them a wider world. Some fortunate kids get to go to high-priced summer camps where a degree of learning can happen in a context of relaxation and fun. And kids of all economic strata can pursue the sort of eccentric and self-determined projects for which there simply isn't time during the traditional academic year, but which often turn out to be nourishing and memorable.

I myself remember fondly a summer spent scavenging spare bicycle parts, which a friend and I then cobbled together into what we called Frankenbikes. Our plan was to sell them, but there were no takers for our bizarre creations. Still, I got pretty handy with a wrench and also learned a valuable lesson: I'd think long and hard before ever again working on a product for which there was no conceivable demand.

Such idylls aside, the hard truth is that in terms of learning, the great majority of summer hours are wasted. Kids watch TV or play video games while waiting for their parents to come home from work. Some kids read books; most don't. As for actual academic study, how could that possibly happen? Last year's textbooks have been given back. Teachers are away. Feedback is unavailable. Buildings are locked. Brains are in suspended animation.

How, then, should the school of the future approach the question of summer vacation?

My preferred scenario would be to trade it for a perpetual school experience where vacations can be taken whenever there is a need for one—not too different from what happens in companies. If students are working in multiage groups, all at their own pace, there is no longer an artificial stopping point when you transition to the "next" grade. If your family wants to travel to Europe or you have people coming over for the holidays or you want to start a business, it's not a big deal. Just take the time off. You can't "miss" class, because you're working at your own pace. Even better, you can still do a lot of learning while on the road now that you have access to self-paced videos and exercises. The same flexibility would apply to teachers. Because of the multiteacher environment, teachers could stagger vacations during the year. No one would be asked to give up a restorative break or time for travel, but these would happen without the need of shutting down the entire system.

But okay, I'm a pragmatist and I realize that summer vacation—one of the most sacred of the education establishment's sacred cows—probably isn't going away anytime soon in the majority of schools. Fortunately, computer-based, self-paced mastery learning can solve many of the problems that summer vacation creates.

First of all, Internet-based lessons such as those offered by Khan Academy are always available. The Internet doesn't close for the summer! Motivated kids can continue advancing and reviewing. Their minds stay active, their neurons keep firing.

This leaves the question of teacher help and feedback. As we've seen in the discussion of the Los Altos pilot program, the Academy has, with the help of experienced classroom teachers, developed a sophisticated feedback dashboard to give teachers real-time information regarding students' progress and difficulties. The dashboard doesn't need a school building in order to be accessed; there is no reason why teachers couldn't continue to monitor student work and serve as online tutors during the summer. This would basically be an updated version of "summer school," though with far lower cost than the current version—and with far greater mobility available to both students and teachers.

The Future of Transcripts

Given that we live in a competitive and increasingly interconnected world, and given that there will always be more applicants than slots available for the finest schools, how do we decide who gets to go to Harvard or Oxford or Heidelberg, or, for that matter, the leading universities in Taipei, Bologna, or São Paulo?

Given that there are not enough resources available to give every person extensive postgraduate training in his or her first choice of career, how do we decide who gets to be a doctor or an architect or an engineer?

Given that the most desirable job openings will always be met by a multiplicity of candidates, how do we decide who gets the gig or the promotion? Who should become the leader whose skill and character will in turn affect the livelihoods and morale of many other people?

These are bedeviling questions. They've always been bedeviling questions, and have become even more so as school applications are less and less limited by national borders and as corporations scour the entire globe for the best minds, the most creative thinkers, and the most motivated workers. How do you compare one applicant to another when they grew up in different cultures, speaking different languages, with widely divergent economic standing and, in turn, the various opportunities or lack thereof that go with wealth or poverty? How can you settle the question of which academic or personal criteria really matter as predictors of success? In the name of fairness and also practicality, how can you be confident that you're comparing apples to apples?

Conventional education has done a woefully inadequate job of even asking these questions, let alone answering them.

How do conventional schools appraise their students? The first way, of course, is by letter grades. Could anything be less precise, less meaningful, or more capricious? As everybody knows, all schools have "easy markers" and "hard markers." If standards can vary widely on either side of a hallway or a row of lockers, how much less uniform will they be from state to state or nation to nation? Yet letter grades are where the rankings start. Combined into that serious- and objective-sounding statistic called the grade point average, letter grades take on a seeming legitimacy and a determinative power well in excess of their reliability. If the individual grades are hazy and subjective, why should we imagine that their composite is precise and scientific? GPA is at best a blunt instrument. True, it can provide a general idea of whether a kid showed up, engaged with school, and played the game. But it is sheer blindness and folly to imagine that GPA alone tells you much about a student's intelligence or creativity. Does someone with a 3.6 necessarily have more to offer to the world than someone with a 3.2? I wouldn't bet on it.

Then there are the standardized tests to which students are subjected from third grade straight on through to grad school. As I've said, I am not antitesting; I believe that well-conceived, well-designed, and fairly administered tests constitute one of our few real sources of reliable and relatively objective data regarding students' preparedness. But note that I say *preparedness*, not potential. Well-designed tests can give a pretty solid idea of what a student has learned, but only a very approximate picture of what she *can* learn. To put it in a slightly different way, tests tend to measure quantities of information (and sometimes knowledge) rather than quality of minds—not to mention character. Besides, for all their attempts to appear precise and comprehensive, test scores seldom identify truly notable ability. If you're the admissions director at Caltech or in charge of hiring engineers at Apple, you're going to see a heck of a lot of candidates who had perfect scores on their math SATs. They are all going to be fairly smart people, but the scores tell you little about who is truly unique.

Tacitly acknowledging the inadequacy of grades and testing as measures of ability or worthiness, many schools and employers also use extracurricular activities, third-party recommendations, and applicant-written essays as part of the selection process. In principle, this is a good thing, as it moves beyond snapshot moments and seeks insight into applicants as flesh-and-blood individuals. The obvious problem, though, is that the game is rigged in favor of those who understand how to work the system. These tend to be families that are already educated, well connected, or wealthy. Children of doctors, professors, and engineers have access to people whom they can do research under. Students who have parents, siblings, or cousins who have attended selective education programs get coaching on how to optimize their chances. A kid whose family friends include CEOs and legislators will tend to have more articulate and impressive recommenders than a kid who comes from a blue-collar family. Does any of this say anything significant about the applicant himself? Even on the so-called personal essays, students from wealthy or particularly ambitious families sometimes have help from well-paid counselors and consultants...who give them tips on how to sound sincere! Good luck to the overworked admissions officer who has to thread her way between the heartfelt and the cleverly bogus.

How then, in my thought experiment school of the future, would I appraise both the performance and the potential of my students?

First, I would eliminate letter grades altogether. In a system based on mastery learning, there is no need and no place for them. Students advance only when they demonstrate clear proficiency with a concept, as measured either by the ten-in-a-row heuristic or some future refinement of it. Since no one is pushed ahead (or left behind) *until* proficiency is reached, the only possible grade would be an A. To paraphrase Garrison Keillor, all the kids would be *way* above average, so grades would be pointless.

In pursuit of the elusive ideal of comparing apples to apples, I would keep some version of standardized testing, though with several significant changes. I would alter the content of the tests from year to year far more than is currently done, include richer tasks, and attempt to incorporate an open-ended design component; this would limit the appeal of test-prep factories and in turn lessen the unfair advantage held by kids from wealthy families. The emphasis of the exam would also not be a one-time snapshot, but something that could and should be retaken after refining one's skills (more affluent students already treat the SAT this way). And in recognition of the hard truth that standardized tests will never be perfect, I would put far less emphasis on them than is currently the case.

Instead, I would propose, as the centerpieces of student appraisal, two things: *a running, multiyear narrative* not only of what a student has learned but how she learned it; and a portfolio of a student's creative work.

As we saw in the discussion of the Los Altos pilot program, readily available technology gives us the ability to track students' progress, work habits, and problem-solving methods in unprecedented detail. The software needed to do so can be customized to the particular needs of any school, and is becoming more sophisticated all the time. The simplest part of the available feedback is quantitative: How far did a student go in math? How many concepts did he master in a given length of time? Is she above or below the median level for her age?

While this information is important, the far more interesting element of the feedback is *qualitative*. This is where tremendous progress remains to be made—a very exciting prospect for the very near future. Aside from counting concepts and measuring time, what can we *infer* from a student's efforts at Khan Academy or some other version of computer-based education? What can we learn about his or her work ethic, persistence, resilience—elements of character that are at least as important as sheer intelligence as predictors of success? Johnny gets stuck. Does he flee the frustration by putting in less time, or does he dig in and work harder until he's figured it out? Sally goes through a patch where her progress is labored and slow. Does she bounce back from it or give in to discouragement and waning confidence? As a seventh grader, Mo seems disengaged and puts in very little time at lessons. As a ninth grader he's spending hours on biology; what does this say about his growing maturity and his possible gift for a particular field?

Clearly, this sort of information, if carefully interpreted, gives us a far more three-dimensional picture of a student than does a bunch of letter grades and numerical scores; it gives us a picture not just of a test-taker, but a *learner.*

I can also envision a category of data that would track a characteristic currently altogether ignored in student assessment but hugely desirable either on a college campus or in a workplace: the ability and willingness to help others.

The large and mixed-age classes I envision would be learning environments in which an important part would be played by peer-to-peer tutoring. And part of the running narrative of every student's educational career should make reference to that, should record and honor not only the time and effort put in on one's own behalf but also the work done on behalf of other people. Software could easily be developed to track this, and I believe the data would be valuable. A generous student will grow into a generous colleague. Someone who communicates well in school will likely communicate well in life. People who are skilled at explaining concepts to others probably understand them deeply.

If I were an admissions officer or a personnel director, I

would love to have some insight into candidates' tendencies in terms of their willingness to help, to give, to pursue not only their own goals but the general good of a community or team. A multiyear, data-based narrative—privacy-protected, of course, and made available only to people of the student's choosing—would present a compelling and many-sided preview of how an applicant would be likely to function and contribute in the world.

This brings me to the idea of the "creative portfolio" as a central part of a student's "transcript." Everyone is beginning to recognize that curiosity and creativity are more important attributes than a mere facility for a particular subject; yet except for narrowly defined art schools, few institutions even consider an applicant's creative output. This is doubly wrong. First, it implies that only "art" is creative—a view that is provincial and limiting. Science, engineering, and entrepreneurship are equally creative. Second, if we fail to take a serious look at what students have created *on their own*, above and beyond lessons and tests, we miss an opportunity to appreciate what is truly special about them. More than any data, grades, or assessment, someone's actual creative product is the best testament of his or her ability to create from scratch, to make a solution out of an open-ended problem.

Serving the Underserved

Let me remind you of the mission statement that has guided Khan Academy since day one: To provide a free, world-class education for anyone, anywhere.

Admittedly, this is a rather grandiose ambition. It probably springs at least in part from the fact that I myself am the child of immigrants and I have seen with my own eyes places like Bangladesh, India, and Pakistan, where the inadequacy and unfair distribution of educational opportunity is a scandal and a tragedy (and pre-Katrina New Orleans wasn't much better). But if my internationalist perspective is partly a function of personal history and emotion, it is also a matter of simple practicality. We live on a small planet, in a world that, as Thomas Friedman put it, is "hot, flat, and crowded." A problem in one place—whether that problem is a financial crisis, a political revolution, or a new virus of either the electronic or biological variety—quickly becomes a problem everywhere. Lack of education, and the poverty, hopelessness, and unrest that tend to go with it, are therefore not local issues but global ones. The world needs all the trained minds and bright futures it can get, and it needs them everywhere.

As a parent myself, I completely understand the human tendency to regard one's own kids as the most precious in the universe. To every mother and every father, of course they are; biology takes care of that. But there is a somewhat dangerous corollary to this natural parental love. Sometimes it seems that, both as individuals and as societies, we think it's okay to be selfish as long as it's on behalf of the kids. Clearly, there's a hypocrisy here; we're still serving the interests of our own DNA and our own narrow clan. We give ourselves a free pass on something that is emotionally right but morally wrong. As long as *our* kids are getting educated, we won't worry about the kids a block, or a nation, or a continent away. But are we really doing our kids a favor by taking this isolationist, me-first position? I don't think so. I think we're condemning them to live in a world of broadening inequality and increasing instability. The better way to help our kids is to help *all* kids.

I believe that computer-based, self-paced learning offers an incredible opportunity toward leveling the playing field all around the world. Contrary to many people's assumptions, it can be delivered very cheaply. It can be deployed in thousands of communities where tens of millions of kids currently have no educational access at all. If computer-based learning has the power to transform education in the developed world, it is potentially even a bigger game-changer in the developing world. Consider an analogy with cell phones. Cell phones have changed life everywhere, but they have positively revolutionized it in the developing world. Why? Because the developing world had so few landlines. For most people there, cell phones aren't just an add-on, they are *it*. As with telephones, so with education—the more egregiously that people were underserved before, the more revolutionary an improvement they will experience.

To be sure, there are daunting challenges in bringing *any* sort of education to the world's poorest and most badly administered places. I do not claim to be an expert in on-the-ground conditions in Africa or Borneo or remote towns in the Andes. But I do know something about the Indian subcontinent, which can, I think, serve as a sort of poster child for the kinds of difficulties to be faced.

In many rural areas, even the most basic prerequisites for education are often missing. Child malnutrition is a huge problem; it's hard to learn on an empty stomach or with maladies that sap strength and concentration. School buildings are few and far between; money for traditional school supplies is hard to find. The skill sets of village kids tend to vary far more widely than even those of the most underserved in the developed world; one twelve-year-old may have somehow managed to attain the same grade level as his middle-class peers in the United States or Europe, while another hasn't even learned to read.

And the list of difficulties goes on. There is a terrible shortage of teachers—and an even bigger shortage of those qualified to teach relatively advanced subjects like trigonometry or physics. Because of vast distances, bad roads, poor communications networks, and administrators who are lax, corrupt, or simply overwhelmed, there is virtually no oversight of school performance, or even teacher attendance. The World Bank estimates that 25 percent of teachers in government primary schools don't come to work on any given day, and only 50 percent of those who do actually teach.[2] Nor is there any reliable way to monitor student work and progress. Is education happening at all in many rural villages? Often it's impossible to know.

These are realities that educators of any stripe must grapple with. But for various reasons I am convinced that software-based, self-paced learning has the best chance of thriving in these sorts of circumstances.

Why? Let's start with cost. If school districts in poor countries can't even afford secondhand textbooks, pencils, and blackboard erasers, how can they possibly afford up-to-the-minute video lessons? The answer is that the lessons, in their most basic form, could be delivered virtually for free.

India loves its Bollywood movies, and even in the most remote rural villages there is almost always someone with a first-generation DVD player and a television set. Thanks to grant money that Khan Academy has received, we already have video lessons translated into Hindi, Urdu, and Bengali (as well as Spanish, Portuguese, and several other languages) and copied onto DVDs, to be distributed free of charge.

Admittedly, just having students *watch* the videos is not ideal; with DVDs alone, they would not be able to do the self-paced exercises or have access to a great deal of feedback. Even so, video lessons on DVD would be a significant improvement over what's available now. Their availability would ameliorate the teacher shortage situation; kids would at least be able to pause, repeat, and review the lessons. And it would be a win—wouldn't it?—if we could give kids in the world's poorest areas even a cheap approximation of what the wealthy have.

But say we aim higher. Say we aim *ridiculously* high. Say we aim to give kids in poor rural villages around the world virtually the same experience as kids in Silicon Valley have. This is preposterous, right? Well, I believe it can be done.

Consider: Inexpensive tablet computers (think of smaller, cheaper iPads) are coming onto the market in India for under $100. If it can be expected to run for around five years, the annual cost of owning this device is $20. As I've already explained, the Khan Academy curriculum is designed so that students can get what they need in one to two hours a day of following lessons and working out problems; this means that a single tablet could be used by four to as many as ten students a day. But let's take the most conservative number; if the computer is shared among four students, the cost is $5 per student per year. Let's now give our students some downtime and some sick days, and posit that the computer is used three hundred days a year. The cost is thus under *two cents per student per day*. Can anyone tell me in good conscience that this is more than the world can afford? Even more, the technology will only get better and cheaper from here on out.

Realistically, cheap tablet devices alone do not suffice to re-create a Silicon Valley–style virtual educational experience. There remain the questions of Internet connectivity and the gathering and use of data regarding students' progress. These are logistical challenges that will vary in different locations, but the general point I want to make is that with some imagination and technological savvy, the challenges can be met far more cheaply than is usually acknowledged.

Without getting too technical, consider Internet access.

Broadband connections would be nice, but broadband is relatively expensive and not currently available everywhere. There are much cheaper alternatives. Bandwidth-hogging videos can be preloaded on devices and user data could be transmitted over cellular networks. If there is no cellular connectivity, information regarding students' work and progress could be downloaded from individual computers, copied onto flash drives, and carried in a *truck* to central servers. They could be carried on a donkey! The point I'm getting at is that not everything in high-tech education has to be high-tech. There are hybrid solutions right in front of us—if we are open to them.

Coming back to cost, cellular Internet connectivity can be had for as little as $2 per month in India. So our per-student expense has now increased to $11 per year ($44 per year per device with Internet that can be shared by four students). Let's further suggest a worst-case scenario in which not even this meager amount can be procured from public or philanthropic funds. What then?

Certainly in a place like India, the price of educating the poor could be covered by the middle class and the well-to-do—not by taxation, charity, or under any sort of compulsion, but by giving prosperous families themselves a much better deal on education.

Let me explain. In much of the developing world, especially in both South and East Asia, school is regarded not primarily as a place to learn—the rigid conditions don't allow for much of that—but rather as a place to show off what you know. The actual learning happens before or after school, through the use of private tutors. Even middle-class families tend to see tutors as a necessary expense, and private tutoring is in fact how many teachers actually end up making something approaching a middle-class income. As teachers of advanced subjects are in short supply, so are tutors in those subjects. Accordingly, tutoring in calculus or chemistry gets pretty pricey.

What if the families who currently use private tutors were offered an alternative that was far less expensive, far more comprehensive, and designed up to a proven international standard? In other words, what if they were offered paid but low-cost access to computer centers that offered Internet-based, self-paced mastery learning? This might be bad news for the private tutors, but it would be good news for everybody else. Middle-class families would spend far less for quality education; kids would have the benefit of a complete, tested curriculum rather than the hit-or-miss of tutors whose own understanding might be less than world-class.

Supported by the fees of those who could afford them, the centers would be free to the poor and the currently unschooled. The beauty is that the middle-class kids, still attending conventional classes, would use the center in the early morning or the evening. The kids (and adults for that matter) without access to other education could use the facilities during the day.

Now, as a sworn enemy of one-size-fits-all approaches, I'm not suggesting that this scheme would work everywhere or that it couldn't be improved upon. But I am convinced that the basic model—providing high-quality, low-cost education to the affluent and middle class and using the revenues to make the same services free to the poor—has a place in how we finance our educational future. In a perfect world, such schemes would not be necessary; governments and societies would see to it that all had access to quality education. In the real world, however, with its blatant inequities and tragic shortfalls in both money and ideas, new approaches are needed to prop up and refresh a tired system that works for some but fails for many. The cost of wasting millions of minds is simply unacceptable.

The Future of Credentials

When people talk about education, they are usually mixing together several ideas. The first is the idea of teaching and learning. That is what the bulk of this book is about—how can we rethink the best ways to learn. The second is the idea of socialization. That, too, we have touched on when discussing peer-to-peer collaboration and mixed-age classrooms. The third is the idea of credentialing—giving a piece of paper to someone that proves to the world that they know what they know. These three different aspects of education are muddled together because today they are all performed by the same institutions—you go to college to learn, have a life experience, and get a degree.

Let's try a simple thought experiment: What if we were to separate (or decouple) the teaching and credentialing roles of universities? What would happen if regardless of where (or whether) you went to college, you could take rigorous, internationally recognized assessments that measured your understanding and proficiency in various fields—anything from quantum physics to European history to software engineering. Some could be assessments designed in conjunction with employers looking for people with particular skills. Because these assessments could be even more thorough than what happens during exam time at many universities, they might be expensive, maybe $300 a pop. You could also take these exams at any age.

Think about the implications. Most students who go to college are not going to nationally known private colleges like Princeton or Rice or Duke. They are also not going to well-known state universities like Berkeley, UT Austin, or the University of Michigan. The great majority of students go to not-well-known regional or community colleges. This is especially the case for students from underrepresented communities because these schools have more open admissions and tend to be more affordable (although they can still be quite expensive). Even if a student gets an amazing education at these schools they are at a marked disadvantage. Because employers use the "difficulty of getting in" to a school as a proxy for the quality of its graduates, the students from less well-known schools often fail to pass the résumé screen. College is all about opening up opportunity, but the reality is that the ultra-smart, ultra-hardworking kid from a poor family, who worked full-time while getting good grades at a regional school or community college, will almost always be passed over when compared to someone graduating from a more well-known and selective school.

With our hypothetical assessments—microcredentials if you will—anyone could prove that they know just as much in a specific domain as someone with an exclusive diploma. Even more, they wouldn't have had to go into debt and attend university to prove it. They could prepare through textbooks, the Khan Academy, or tutorials from a family member. Because even name-brand diplomas give employers limited information, it would be a way for even elite college graduates to differentiate themselves from their peers, to show that they actually have retained deep, useful skills. In short, it would make the credential that most students and parents need cheaper (since it is an assessment that is not predicated on seat time in lecture halls) and more powerful—it would actually tell employers who is best ready to contribute at their organizations based on metrics that they find important.

Now, I do not think this will eliminate the need or value of universities for many students. If you are lucky enough to attend a good university, you will be immersed in a community of inspiring peers and professors doing amazing things. You will build social bonds that are at least as valuable— emotionally and economically—as that first job out of college. You will have life experiences that are priceless. The universities themselves will continue to conduct cutting-edge research that pushes society forward (and in which undergrads can often participate). The signal to employers of getting in and being socialized in these types of communities will always carry weight. College will become something similar to an MBA. It will be optional. You can have a very successful career without it, but it is a great life experience that will probably help if you can afford the time and money.

What this will change is the opportunities and the ecosystem for the great majority of students who aren't given the luxury to attend a name-brand school, because now they'd have the opportunity to—at minimum—work toward a recognized credential in whatever way they see fit. It would allow a forty-year-old laid-off factory worker to show that they still have the analytical skills and brain plasticity to work alongside twenty-two-year-old college grads in a twenty-first-century job. It would allow anyone, in any field, to better themselves and prepare for valuable credentials without the sacrifice of money and time that today's higher education demands.

What College Could Be Like

I have never let my schooling interfere with my education.
—MARK TWAIN

In the last section, we explored what would happen if credible credentials could be earned outside of a college. I'd like to turn now to a vision of how college education might change to better suit our needs. The starting point for this discussion is a very basic disconnect between most students' expectations for college—a means to employment first and a good intellectual experience second—and what universities believe their value is—an intellectual and social experience first, with only secondary consideration to employment.

And it is unfair to expect traditional universities to cater to the whims of the economy or job market. They are designed to be places insulated from the "real world" so that intellectual truth and pure research can be pursued with as few practical constraints as possible. This is what allows them to be truly fertile soil for breakthrough ideas and fundamental discoveries. Even more, some professors—especially those at large research universities—don't view teaching as the best use of their time, and were not selected to be professors based on teaching ability. They were hired to do research and sometimes view teaching as a necessary evil. I have professor friends who feel lucky when they don't have to teach a course at all.

So let us face this as an open-ended design problem—is it possible to craft a university experience that bridges the gap between students' expectations and professors' inclinations? One that provides the rich social and intellectual atmosphere of a good existing college, while at the same time exposing students to those intellectual but also practical fields that will make them valuable to the world? Where the faculty is invested in the future of their students and not just their own ability to publish research papers? And now let's be ambitious: Might there be a sustainable way to make this experience free, or even pay the students to participate?

Computer science is a good place to start. I know the field reasonably well and I also have a sense for the job market—which is tight and growing tighter every day. It is a field where degrees can be valuable, but the ability to design and execute on open-ended, complex projects is paramount; seventeen-year-olds with unusual creativity and intellect have been known to get six-figure salaries. Because of the demand for talent and the recognition that college degrees and high GPAs are not the best predictor of creativity, intellect, or passion, top employers have begun to treat summer internships as something of a farm league. They observe students actually working and make offers to those who perform the best. Employers know that working with a student is an infinitely better assessment than any degree or transcript.

Students have also begun to recognize something very counterintuitive: that they are more likely to get an intellectual grasp of computer science—which is really the logical and algorithmic side of mathematics—by working at companies like Google, Microsoft, or Facebook than by reading textbooks or sitting in lecture halls. They see the projects that these companies give their interns as being more intellectually challenging and open-ended than the somewhat artificial projects given in classrooms. Even more, they know that the product of their efforts will touch millions of people instead of just being graded by a teaching assistant and thrown away.

So, to be clear, in software engineering, the internship has become far more valuable to the students as an intellectual learning experience than any university class. And it has become more valuable to the employer as a signal of student ability than any formal credential, class taken, or grade point average.

I want to emphasize that these internships are very different from the ones that many people remember having even twenty years ago. There is no getting coffee for the boss, sorting papers, or doing other types of busywork. The projects aren't just cute things to work on that have no impact on real people. In fact, the best way to differentiate between forward-looking, twenty-first-century industries and old-school, backward-looking ones is to see what interns are doing. At top Internet companies, interns might be creating patentable artificial intelligence algorithms or even creating new lines of business. By contrast, at a law firm, government office, or publishing house, they will be doing paperwork, scheduling meetings, and proofreading text. This menial work will be paid accordingly, if at all, whereas pay scales at the new-style internships reflect the seriousness of the work involved; college interns in Silicon Valley can earn over $20,000 for the summer.

Given the increasing importance of internships in terms of both intellectual enrichment and enhancement of job prospects, why do traditional colleges limit them only to summers, pushing them aside to cater to the calendar needs of lectures and homework? The answer is simple inertia—this is how it has always been done, so people haven't really questioned it.

Actually, some universities have. Despite being founded not even sixty years ago, the University of Waterloo is generally considered to be Canada's top engineering school. Walk down a hallway at Microsoft or Google and you will find as many Waterloo grads as those from MIT, Stanford, or Berkeley— despite the fact that, because of work visa issues, it is a significant hassle for American employers to hire Canadian nationals. And this isn't some attempt to get low-cost labor from across the border—Waterloo graduates are commanding salaries as high as the very best American grads. What is Waterloo doing right?

For one thing, Waterloo recognized the value of internships long ago (they call them co-ops) and has made them an integral part of its students' experience. By graduation, a typical Waterloo grad will have spent six internships lasting a combined twenty-four months at major companies—often American. The typical American grad will have spent about thirty-six months in lecture halls and a mere three to six months in internships.

This past winter—not summer—all of the interns at the Khan Academy, and probably most of the interns in Silicon Valley, were from Waterloo because that is the only school that views internships as an integral part of students' development *outside of the summer*. While the students at most colleges are taking notes in lecture halls and cramming for winter exams, the Waterloo students are pushing themselves intellectually by working on real projects. They are also getting valuable time with employers and pretty much guaranteeing several job offers once they graduate. On top of that, some are earning enough money during their multiple high-paying internships to pay for their tuition (which is about one-sixth to one-third the cost of a comparable American school) and then some. So Waterloo students graduate with valuable skills, broad intellectual development, high-paying jobs, *and* potential savings after four or five years.

Compare this to the typical American college grad with tens or hundreds of thousands of dollars of debt, no guarantee of an intellectually challenging job, and not much actual experience with which to get a job.

Waterloo has already proven that the division between the intellectual and the useful is artificial; I challenge anyone to argue that Waterloo co-op students are in any way less intellectual or broad-thinking than the political science or history majors from other elite universities. If anything, based on my experience with Waterloo students, they tend to have a more expansive worldview and are more mature than typical new college graduates—arguably due to their broad and deep experience base.

So let us imagine optimizing the model that Waterloo has already begun. Imagine a new university in Silicon Valley—it doesn't have to be here but it will help to make things concrete. I am a big believer that inspiring physical spaces and rich community really do elevate and develop one's thinking. So we'll put in dormitories, nicely manicured outdoor spaces, and as many areas that facilitate interaction and collaboration as possible. Students would be encouraged to start clubs and organize intellectual events. So far, this is not so different from your typical residential college.

What is completely different is where and how the students spend their days. Rather than taking notes in lecture halls, these students will be actively learning through real-world intellectual projects. A student could spend five months at Google optimizing a search algorithm. She might spend another six months at Microsoft working on human speech recognition. The next four months could be spent apprenticing under a designer at Apple, followed by a year of building her own mobile applications. Six months could be spent doing biomedical research at a start-up or even at another university like Stanford. Another four months could be spent prototyping and patenting an invention. Students could also apprentice with venture capitalists and successful entrepreneurs, eventually leading to attempts to start their own businesses. One of the primary roles of the college itself would be to make sure that the internships are challenging and intellectual; that they truly do support a student's development.

All of this will be tied together with a self-paced academic scaffold through something like the Khan Academy. Students will also still be expected to have a broad background in the arts and deep proficiency in the sciences; it will just be done in a more natural way. They will be motivated to formally learn about linear algebra when working on a computer graphics apprenticeship at Pixar or Electronic Arts. They will want to learn accounting when working under the CFO of a publicly traded company. Ungraded seminars will be held regularly during nights and weekends when students can enjoy and discuss great works of literature and art. If the students decide that they want to prove their academic ability within a domain—like algorithms or French history—they can sign up for the rigorous assessments we discussed in the last chapter.

Let me stress the notion of ungraded seminars in the arts, because I think it would lead to more appreciation of the humanities than what goes on in traditional colleges. Take a look at literature. In most colleges and high schools, students are forced to read great works—or at least those deemed great by their professors. They do this within a deadline-based setting where they have to read two hundred pages by Friday. And this is while they have a lot of other work to do from their other classes. At the end of the reading, they must participate in a discussion or take an exam or write a paper—which is graded. Given all of this artificial structure and assessment around a work of literature, do we really think the student has time to appreciate and enjoy it? Is the point here really to see who can read two hundred pages by Friday and impress a professor on an essay to get an A? Look at the graduates who used their straight A's in comparative literature, history, or political science to get a competitive position in investment banking, law, medicine, or consulting. How much do they remember, much less read and appreciate, the classics now? Many of the ones I know haven't read a major work of literature since college.

I feel strongly about this because when I was in school I was not a fan of the forced reading for a paper and/or exam around an artificial timeline. It made me, and my peers, treat amazing works of art as busywork that was standing between us and our grades/diplomas/jobs. We've already talked about how forcing math down students' throats according to an artificially imposed one-pace-fits-all curriculum causes them to dislike it. It is even worse in the humanities. One can appreciate and internalize neither logarithms nor Thoreau if they are force-fed at an artificial pace. This is why so many students—often boys—have something approaching post-traumatic stress disorder when someone brings up *Wuthering Heights* or *Moby Dick*. When Newton or Gauss explored mathematics that unlocked mysteries of their universe, their intent was to empower—and maybe inspire—humanity. The goals of Twain, Dickens, or Austen were similar: to deeply entertain while opening our eyes and minds. Neither the great mathematicians' nor the great writers' goal was to create tools of torture for high school or college students—but that is how many students have grown to view their work.

One of my all-time favorite books is Jane Austen's *Pride and Prejudice*—I know, a bit girly, but great is great. I hated the book when I was forced to read it and write a book report at fourteen. I only realized that I loved it—and a lot of literature—when I reread it for fun on a whim when I was twenty-three. The same is true for *Huckleberry Finn*, *A Tale of Two Cities*, and *Brave New World*. Not only was I more mature and had more perspective on life, but I had the time and motivation to appreciate it. I believe that motivation, the culture of a community, and outlets for exploration drive the appreciation of the arts, not grades and credit-unit requirements.

Returning to our hypothetical apprenticeship-based college in Silicon Valley: Who will be the faculty? Why not the executives, scientists, artists, designers and engineers that the students will work with? Some of the most effective professors I have had in my education were not professional researchers; they were retired or practicing scientists, engineering, investors, or executives, all of whom *wanted* to teach and mentor.

Traditional universities proudly list the Nobel laureates they have on campus (most of whom have little to no interaction with students). Our university would list the great entrepreneurs, inventors, and executives serving as student advisers and mentors. This could be supplemented with dedicated faculty with more specialized backgrounds in fields like history or law or literature or mathematics.

What about grades and a transcript? How will employers and graduate schools know which students are strong and which are weak? As already touched on, many of the employers will have had direct interaction with these students through their apprenticeships, giving them a much deeper view into a student's abilities, work ethic, and personality. Even employers—or graduate schools—who have not had direct interaction with the student can see the student's portfolio of work, and also, if the student allows, can have access to letters of assessment and recommendation from people the student has worked with. This is essentially how any job applicant is treated five years after graduation today—grades and majors take a backseat to what the individual has actually done in the real world. Additionally, students will be free to take the aforementioned rigorous assessments to show that they can go deep in certain academic areas.

Will the traditional GPA be missed as a measure of ability? I don't think so. Consider that the average graduating GPA at many elite universities is around a 3.5.[3] Couple that with the fact that 95 to 97 percent of students graduate and you may conclude that the most difficult part of getting a degree with a decent GPA from some universities is getting through their hyperintense admissions process when you are seventeen. The rest gets pretty fuzzy.

I am by no means the first person to rethink what college could be. PayPal cofounder and Facebook investor Peter Thiel has been a vocal critic of what he calls a "college bubble" and has funded the Thiel Fellowship program to pop it. Thiel Fellows, as they are called, are twenty high-caliber students who are each given $100,000 to drop out of college and work on an ambitious idea or project. According to the program's website, the fellows will be "mentored by our network of visionary thinkers, investors, scientists, and entrepreneurs, who provide guidance and business connections that can't be replicated in any classroom." What I love about this is that it is mixing things up and making people realize that the traditional way isn't necessarily the best way for everyone.

The difference between the Thiel Fellowship and what I am advocating is that I do not want to throw out the idea of college entirely. I think the shared experience of being on a campus and exploring alongside other motivated and inquisitive individuals is a powerful one. It is also clear that for most students a college degree is a form of risk mitigation, something that's there to fall back on. Many of the Thiel Fellows may not succeed on their first big venture. The prestige of having been a Thiel Fellow may open future doors, but this cannot be guaranteed. Still, allowing for some differences, the Thiel program and my own vision are aligned in spirit. Grow Thiel's fellowship to several hundred students a year; allow them to be mentored in various settings, not just one where they are starting a venture; house the students in an inspiring residential campus; and give them a scaffold of academics, and we are talking about almost the same thing.

We started this thought experiment by envisioning a school focused on engineering, design, and entrepreneurship in Silicon Valley. We placed it there so that it could take advantage of the local ecosystem. Why not a school of finance or journalism located in New York or London, or a school focused on energy in Houston? Even better, why can't they all be affiliated so that a student can experience multiple cities and industries, all while having a residential and intellectual support network?

Will this be for everyone? Absolutely not. But majoring in literature or accounting at a traditional university isn't for everyone either. There should be more options, and this could be one of them—an option that introduces diversity of thought and practice into a higher education world that has not changed dramatically in hundreds of years.

It also should be noted that this doesn't necessarily have to be a new university. Existing campuses could move in this direction by deemphasizing or eliminating lecture-based courses, having their students more engaged in research and co-ops in the broader world, and having more faculty with broad backgrounds who show a deep desire to mentor students.

Conclusion
Making Time for Creativity

Here is one of the most ancient questions in the history of education: Can creativity be taught?

No one yet has come up with a definitive answer to that riddle, and I certainly don't presume to offer one here. But I will say this: Whether or not creativity, still less genius, can be taught, it can certainly be squelched. And our current factory model of education seems perversely designed to do exactly that.

Nearly everything about our current system rewards passivity and conformity and discourages differentness and fresh thinking. For most of the conventional school day, kids just sit while teachers talk. Cloistered away with students their own age, they are deprived of the varying and often mind-stretching perspectives of kids both more and less advanced. They move in lockstep through rigid, balkanized curricula aimed less at deep learning than at the fulfillment of government mandates and creditable performance on standardized tests.

If this lockstep education inculcates a chilling fear of

falling behind, an even more insidious outcome is that it also undermines the whole idea of moving ahead. Why learn what you won't be tested on? Why go where the overworked and stressed-out teacher won't have the time or energy to follow? Thus initiative is frowned upon, making it clear that conventional education—whatever the political slogans happen to say—is not about excellence; it's about minimizing risk, eliminating downside surprises. Inevitably, however, the upside is muted as well. In this straitjacket of a system, the successful student—the student who gets A's—is the one who does the expected thing, who plows dutifully ahead on the path of least resistance. Does it take a measure of intelligence and discipline to succeed along this narrow path? Yes, of course it does. Does it call for any sort of originality or specialness? Probably not.

Even our usual extracurricular activities tend to encourage an orderly plodding along predictable paths. In the name of making kids well rounded—which of course is code for *attractive to admissions officers*—we present them with a menu that is illusory in its actual range of options. It's a bit like the 500-channel TV scenario; how much is real choice and how much is just clutter? In the standard view, everyone should play a sport. Everyone should have something brainy, like chess club or debating team, on his or her transcript. And let's not forget the artsy side of life. Drama club? Marching band?

To be clear, I am not trying to denigrate the intrinsic value of any of these pastimes; if a kid feels a true calling toward chess or trumpet playing or set design, I think that's great. What I'm criticizing is an educational approach that, because of its built-in inefficiencies and obsession with control, keeps kids so busy, often with activities that have nothing to do with their particular talents or interests, that they have no time to *think*. There's a cruel irony in this. Pressured to keep a full plate of purportedly enriching activities, kids end up barely noticing that their interior lives—their uniqueness, curiosity, and creativity—are in fact becoming impoverished.

To hit the point home, in 2001 the dean of admissions at an elite university asked a group of students, "What do you daydream about?" One kid told her, "We don't daydream. There's no reward for it, so we don't do it."[4]

In this connection, let's consider the Plato quote that serves as an epigraph for this book:

> The elements of instruction…should be presented to the mind in childhood, but not with any compulsion. Knowledge which is acquired under compulsion has no hold on the mind. Therefore do not use compulsion, but let early education be rather a sort of amusement; this will better enable you to find out the natural bent of the child.

Discovering—and nurturing—the natural bent of the child; isn't this the proper goal of education? And what exactly is meant by this vague phrase "natural bent"? To me, it refers to the particular mix of talents and perspectives that makes each mind unique, and that allows for some minds to be strikingly original. This originality is related to intelligence, but not identical to it. It correlates with differentness and not infrequently with strangeness. Originality is stubborn but not indestructible.

You can't tell it what to do, and if you try too hard to steer it, you either chase it away or murder it.

But can you *teach* it? Frankly, I doubt this. Yet at the same time I am entirely confident that more creativity would *emerge* from my imagined school of the very near future. My reasons for believing this are not at all mysterious. More creativity would emerge because it would be *allowed* to emerge and because there would be *time* for this to happen.

Let's think a moment about this deceptively simple issue of time. The conventional school day burns up roughly half of students' waking hours; conventional homework commandeers another significant chunk. During all this time, kids' concentration and effort are directed toward achieving entirely predictable results. They're working the same problems as everybody else, trying to get to the same and only right answer. They're all writing basically the same essay, memorizing the same names and dates. In other words, they are spending more than half their waking hours being the *opposite* of creative.

As I hope is clear by now, I'm a big believer that almost *anyone* can obtain an intuitive understanding of almost any concept if he or she approaches it with a deep understanding of the fundamentals. Students need a firm foundation before anything of consequence can be accomplished. But the simple truth is that building this foundation doesn't need to eat up half their lives. Using self-paced video lessons, in combination with the computer-based feedback and team-teaching help already described, fundamental coursework can be handled in one or two hours a day. That frees up five or six or seven hours for creative pursuits, both individual and collaborative. That might mean writing poems or computer code, making films or build-ing robots, working with paint or in some weird little corner of physics or math—it being remembered that original math or science or engineering is neither more nor less than art by another name.

If the sheer grinding length of the conventional school day is a brake on creativity, so is the artificial chopping up of time into lessons. Time, after all, is a continuum; like thought itself, it flows. The end of a series of lessons blocks the flow, puts a brick wall in the way. It tells students where they need to stop learning. This is bad enough in cases where a student, say, might like to look a bit more deeply into the causes of the French Revolution; where it's really deadly, however, is in cases where a student is off on a daring and creative tangent, wres-tling with a major project or an idea that is truly novel. That kind of creative work simply can't be put on a deadline; genius doesn't punch a time clock! Can you imagine if someone told Einstein, *Okay, wrap up this relativity thing, we're moving on to European history*? Or said to Michelangelo, *Time's up for the ceiling, now go paint the walls*. Yet versions of this snuffing out of creativity and boundary-stretching thought happen all the time in conventional schools.

The schoolhouse I envision would be very different in this regard. Because I would stress the connections and the conti-nuity among concepts, there would be no brick walls between one "subject" and the next. Since learning would be self-paced and self-motivated, there would be no ticking clock telling stu-dents when they had to drop a particular line of inquiry. And since the higher goal of our school would be deep, conceptual understanding rather than mere test prep, students would be given the time and latitude to follow their curiosity as far as it would carry them. Thus my belief that creativity would emerge because it would be *allowed* to emerge.

But there's a corollary to this that makes a lot of people nervous. *If you allow and encourage true creativity, you also have to accept the possibility of failure.* A student might pursue an esoteric math topic for a year and never find an answer. A fresh approach to an engineering problem might obsess a student for many months then turn out not to work. A student playwright might never figure out his final act, student poetry might turn out just plain bad. My response to these failures: So what? Think what was learned along the way. Honor the effort and the courage that went into these ambitious and often solitary undertakings. Think about the grand results that *might* have happened—that can *only* happen when people pursue big ideas and take big risks. Going back to the very beginning of this book, one of the many things that has made America the most fertile soil for innovation is that it does not stigmatize risk and failure anywhere near as much as the rest of the world. Our schools should be the same—environments for safe experimentation, viewing failure as an opportunity for learning rather than a mark of shame.

Unfortunately, our educational establishment seems to have an abiding fear and hatred of failure, to regard it as a dirty word. In a world of letter grades, a D or an F is a stain; under a system of brittle benchmarks and politically motivated incentives, a "failure" carries a stigma and a penalty. So we lower our standards and water down our expectations in the illusory hope of bringing "success" within the reach of all. But this attitude is both hypocritical and condescending. Not only does it drain the meaning from the true ideal of excellence, but it completely fails to grasp the value of aiming high, even if the result is falling short. Our world needs bold thinking and innovative approaches. Those things are much more likely to be offshoots of big failures than of small, safe, and predictable successes.

Accordingly, the school I envision would be a place where mistakes are allowed, tangents are encouraged, and big thinking is celebrated as a *process*—whatever the outcome might turn out to be. This is no magic formula to make kids more creative; rather, it's a way to give light and space and time to the creativity that already exists in each of us—and that, in some mysterious few who will go on to change the world, rises to the level of genius.

So then, I hope I've clearly presented at least a basic outline of what my imagined One World Schoolhouse would look like and how it would work. It would be inclusive; it would be affordable. It would help to level the educational playing field both within communities and across national borders.

The school I envision would embrace technology not for its own sake, but as a means to improve deep conceptual understanding, to make quality, relevant education far more portable, and—somewhat counterintuitively—to humanize the classroom. It would raise both the status and the morale of teachers by freeing them from drudgery and allowing them more time to *teach*, to help. It would give students more independence and control, allowing them to claim true ownership of their educations. By mixing ages and encouraging peer-to-peer tutoring, this schoolhouse would give adolescents the chance to begin to take on adult responsibilities.

The schoolhouse would not be the most hushed of places; it would be more like a hive than a chapel. Students needing quiet could seek out private alcoves. But the bigger space would buzz with games and with collaborations. Self-paced rather than lockstep learning would encourage students to share their most recent discoveries about the workings of the universe. Lessons aimed at thorough mastery of concepts—*interrelated* concepts—would proceed in harmony with the way our brains are actually wired, and would prepare students to function in a complex world where *good enough* no longer is.

Yes—a complex world, and an interconnected one. The various outposts of our schoolhouse would therefore be interconnected as well, through things like Skype or Google Hangouts. Students and teachers in San Francisco could interact with those in Toronto, London, or Mumbai. Imagine students in Tehran tutoring students in Tel Aviv or students in Islamabad learning from a professor in New Delhi. Is there really any better way to learn a language or have a global perspective than by regularly interacting with teachers and students around the planet?

In terms of bricks and mortar, the schoolhouse I envision has yet to be built. But the ideas that it is based on have by now been field-tested by millions of online students and tens of thousands more in physical classrooms. The results, whether gathered in anecdotes or measured by hard data, have been extremely gratifying.

For me personally, the biggest discovery has been how hungry students are for real understanding. I sometimes get pushback from people saying, "Well, this is all well and good, but it will only work for *motivated* students." And they say it assuming that maybe 20 percent of students fall into that category. I probably would have agreed with them seven years ago, based on what I'd seen in my own experience with the traditional academic model. When I first started making videos, I thought I was making them only for some subset of students who *cared*— like my cousins or younger versions of myself. What was truly startling was the reception the lessons received from students whom people had given up on, and who were about to give up on themselves. It made me realize that if you give students the opportunity to learn deeply and to see the magic of the universe around them, almost everyone will be motivated.

Teaching methods matter; nuanced feedback and assessment matter. But far more important than any particular set of methods and approaches is the fundamental fact that education has to be continually adapted and improved. The current system is rife with inefficiencies and inequalities, with tragic mismatches between how students are taught and what they need to know; and the situation grows more urgent with every day that the educational status quo survives while the world is changing all around it. This is not an abstract conversation; it's about the futures of real kids, families, communities, and nations.

Is Khan Academy, along with the intuitions and ideas that underpin it, our best chance to move toward a better educational future? That's not for me to say. Other people of vision and goodwill have differing approaches, and I fervently hope that all are given a fair trial in the wider world. But new and bold approaches *do* need to be tried. The one thing we cannot afford to do is to leave things as they are. The cost of inaction is unconscionably high, and it is counted out not in dollars or euros or rupees but in human destinies. Still, as both an engineer and a stubborn optimist, I believe that where there are problems, there are also solutions. If Khan Academy proves to be even part of the solution to our educational malaise, I will feel proud and privileged to have made a contribution.

ACKNOWLEDGMENTS

I would like to thank my wife, Umaima, for loving me and putting up with me; my sister, Farah, for being my first and most influential role model; my mother, Masooda Khan, for everything that a mother does and more; my mother-in-law, Naseem Marvi, for her amazing support; Imran and Diya, for reminding me whom this Khan Academy effort is for; Nadia, for needing help and being willing to work with her crazy cousin; my aunt Nazrat, for believing in me before it was warranted.

A special thanks to Jeremiah Hennessy and Ann Doerr, for seeing potential early on; and Dan Wohl, for being an incredible role model and affording me the balance in life to make Khan Academy a reality.

None of this would be possible without the incredible team at the Khan Academy: Shantanu, Ben, Ben, Ben, Ben (yes, all four), Jason, Bilal, Marcia, Jessica, John, Desmond, Charlotte, Elizabeth, Sundar, Matt, Maureen, Marcos, James, Tom, Minli, Steven, Beth, Chris, Craig, Michael, Kitt, Stephanie, Yun-Fang, Vi, Brit, Esther, Ann, Jonathan, Ted, Larry, Eric and Toby.

I also have an incalculable debt of gratitude to John Doerr,

Bill and Melinda Gates, Reed Hastings, Scott and Signe Cook, and Sean O'Sullivan for believing so strongly in our team and vision.

I thank Richard Pine and Carrie Cook, for convincing me to write a book and guide me through the process. I would also like to thank Cary Goldstein and Brian McLendon at Twelve for their incredible publishing help in turning this into a real book.

Last, but not least, I deeply thank Larry Shames, for being of great assistance in helping shape many, many thoughts and ideas into a coherent narrative.

NOTES

Part 1: Learning to Teach

1. Joan Middendorf and Alan Kalish, "The 'Change-Up' in Lectures," *National Teaching & Learning Forum* 5, no. 2 (1996).
2. R. A. Burns, *Information Impact and Factors Affecting Recall.* Paper presented at Annual National Conference on Teaching Excellence and Conference of Administrators, Austin, Texas (ERIC Document Reproduction Service No. ED 258 639).
3. Margaret Gallagher and P. David Pearson, *Discussion, Comprehension, and Knowledge Acquisition in Content Area Classrooms*, Technical Report No. 480, University of Illinois at Champaign-Urbana, 1989.
4. Benjamin Bloom, "Learning for Mastery," *Evaluation Comment* 1, no. 2 (1968); James Block, *Mastery Learning: Theory and Practice* (New York: Holt, Rinehart & Winston, 1971).
5. T. Guskey and S. Gates, "Synthesis of Research on the Effects of Mastery Learning in Elementary and Secondary Classrooms," *Educational Leadership* 43, no. 8 (1986).
6. D. Levine, *Improving Student Achievement Through Mastery Learning Programs* (San Francisco: Jossey-Bass, 1985).
7. D. Davis and J. Sorrell, "Mastery Learning in Public Schools," *Educational Psychology Interactive* (Valdosta, GA: Valdosta State University, December 1995).
8. Guskey and Gates, "Synthesis of Research."
9. Davis and Sorrell, "Mastery Learning in Public Schools."

Part 2: The Broken Model

1. http://www.ncbi.nlm.nih.gov/pubmed/17616757.

2. Albert J. Harno, *Legal Education in the United States: A Report Prepared for the Survey of the Legal Profession* (San Francisco: Bancroft-Whitney, 1953), 86.

3. "High literacy rates in America...exceeded 90 per cent in some regions by 1800": Hannah Barker and Simon Burrows, eds., *Press, Politics, and the Public Sphere in Europe and North America, 1760–1820* (Cambridge: Cambridge University Press, 2002), 141; for lower rates in Europe, see 9.

4. John Taylor Gatto, "Against School: How Public Education Cripples Our Kids, and Why," *Harper's*, September 2003.

5. Sharon Otterman, "In $32 Million Contract, State Lays Out Some Rules for Its Standardized Tests," *New York Times*, August 12, 2011.

6. Winnie Hu, "New Recruit in Homework Revolt: The Principal," *New York Times*, June 15, 2011.

7. "Do You Have Too Much Homework?" moderated by Holly Epstein Ojalvo, "The Learning Network," *New York Times*, June 16, 2001.

8. Stephen Aloia, "Teacher Assessment of Homework," *Academic Exchange Quarterly* (Fall 2003).

9. National Center for Education Statistics, "Education Indicators: An International Perspective," http://nces.ed.gov/pubs/eiip/eiipid25.asp.

10. Harris Cooper et al., "Does Homework Improve Academic Achievement? A Synthesis of Research, 1987–2003," *Review of Educational Research* 76, no. 1 (Spring 2006).

11. Sandra L. Hofferth and John F. Sandberg, "How American Children Spend Their Time," *Journal of Marriage and Family* 63, no. 2 (May 2001).

12. Jenny Anderson, "Push for A's at Private Schools Is Keeping Costly Tutors Busy," *New York Times*, June 7, 2011.

13. Cathy Davidson, "iPads in the Public Schools," *Duke Today*, January 26, 2011, http://today.duke.edu/2011/01/ipads.html.

Part 3: Into the Real World

1. "Learning Styles Debunked: There Is No Evidence Supporting Auditory and Visual Learning, Psychologists Say," press release, Association for Psychological Science, December 16, 2009, http://www.psychologicalscience.org/index.php/news/releases/learning-styles-debunked-there-is-no-evidence-supporting-auditory-and-visual-learning-psychologists-say.html#hide.
2. Royal Society, *Brain Waves Module 2: Neuroscience: Implications for Education and Lifelong Learning*, Policy document 02/11, February 2011.
3. Marcia L. Conner, "How Adults Learn," http://agelesslearner.com/intros/adultlearning.
4. Malcolm Knowles, *The Adult Learner*, 5th ed. (Woburn, MA: Butterworth-Heinemann, 1998 [originally published 1973]).

Part 4: The One World Schoolhouse

1. Virginia Heffernan, "Education Needs a Digital-Age Upgrade," *New York Times*, August 7, 2011.
2. "Teachers Skipping Work," World Bank, South Asia, http://web.worldbank.org/WBSITE/EXTERNAL/COUNTRIES/SOUTHASIAEXT/0,,contentMDK:20848416~pagePK:146736~piPK:146830~theSitePK:223547,00.html.
3. http://gradeinflation.com/stanford.html.
4. "What Do You Do for Fun? (Extended)," Bloomberg Businessweek, May 24, 2004, http://www.businessweek.com/magazine/content/04_21/b3884138_mz070.htm.

ABOUT TWELVE

TWELVE

TWELVE was established in August 2005 with the objective of publishing no more than twelve books each year. We strive to publish the singular book, by authors who have a unique perspective and compelling authority. Works that explain our culture; that illuminate, inspire, provoke, and entertain. We seek to establish communities of conversation surrounding our books. Talented authors deserve attention not only from publishers, but from readers as well. To sell the book is only the beginning of our mission. To build avid audiences of readers who are enriched by these works—that is our ultimate purpose.

For more information about forthcoming TWELVE books, please go to www.twelvebooks.com.